From Pain to Profit: Secrets of the Peak Performance Trader

Reviews

If you have been trading for any length of time, you have no doubt heard of the rules. For most of us we can apply these rules until one day we toss them aside and find ourselves with disastrous results. Often we blame the departure from our trading plan on news events, family issues, etc. We believe in these rules, but often, we ignore them. Dr. Johnson is right, trading is less about conscious choices than about unconscious programming. Woody gives you the tools to program your unconscious mind. He offers techniques that are sure to resonate with every type of trader. This book will become an essential tool in your trading tool box. A tool to help you discover your limiting beliefs, discharge the negative energies and finally, build a belief structure that supports, not only a trading lifestyle, but every area of your life.

Scott Mangis,

The Human Fund

Managed Forex Accounts

Dr. Johnson has done it. He has written one of the best books on what truly ails traders. Many trading books only mention the psychological barriers that prevent success in the markets. In 'From Pain to Profit: Secrets of the Peak Performance Trader,' you will not only learn how to identify what is holding you back, but simple steps to correct your trading and achieve success. Conquer F.E.A.R. I would recommend reading this book if you plan to be successful in trading any market.

Brandon Wendell, CMT
Instructor / Mentor
Online Trading Academy

Dr. Woody Johnson has managed to put the market place psychology into a proper "frame". Few understand the significance and importance of their own perceptions and belief systems, most of which are false. Woody brings many scenarios to bear that will help the novice see their own foibles and beliefs. This book will help them all to understand themselves better. The market place offers little or no risk – the risk is in the people who attempt to conquer the markets or, more importantly, overcome themselves. The largest roadblock to people's financial success is not their ignorance but their over-optimistic and illusionary view of their knowledge. This book provides a road map through these roadblocks.

Mike Mc Mahon

Director of Education

Online Trading Academy

"In 'From Pain to Profit: Secrets of the Peak Performance Trader' Dr. Johnson hits right at the heart of successful trading: above and beyond all the technical and mechanical skills necessary to win as a trader in such a competitive marketplace, in the end, victory or defeat boils down to the battle within. Dr. Johnson equips us with the tools necessary to prepare for that battle all the way down to the details, so that it is not just the market that we discover and conquer, but ultimately ourselves."

Fernando Gonzalez

XLT- Broad Market Analysis Instructor,

Online Trading Academy

Dr. Johnson's 'From Pain to Profit: Secrets of the Peak Performance Trader' is a must read for any trader. Whether You're a seasoned pro, or a neophyte, this book will help you uncover what's truly needed to succeed in what is one of the most challenging of human endeavors .This book is not about indicators or patterns, but about techniques in mastering your actions, emotions, and getting you to focus on accomplishing your goals. This ultimately is the EDGE everyone seeks, and Dr. Johnson certainly delivers with this narrative.

Gabe Velazquez
OTA Trading Instructor & Mentor

Outstanding.

I have read this at least 4 times. Each time I get something else of value out of it. I think this is very good. And ready for widespread deployment.

JC Coldren
President

Online Trading Academy of Los Angeles

From Pain to Profit: Secrets of the Peak Performance Trader

By

Dr. M. Woodruff Johnson

Dr. M. Woodruff Johnson

From Pain to Profit: Secrets of the Peak Performance Trader

www.peakperformance2k.com

Introduction

"Our lives are not determined by what happens to us but by how we react to what happens, not by what life brings to us, but by the attitude we bring to life. A positive attitude causes a chain reaction of positive thoughts, events, and outcomes. It is a catalyst, a spark that creates extraordinary results." – Anonymous

From Pain to Profit: Secrets of the Peak Performance Trader provides the serious trading professional and the aspiring amateur with high-tech strategies that promote maximum effectiveness and peak performance while trading in challenging and changing financial markets. This book will teach you:

- To keenly focus your efforts

- To adopt "an edge of quiet desperation" in making successful investments and trades.

- To commit to following your plan and your rules.

- To overcome the specter of fear, greed, and self-doubt by harnessing your passion for following your rules

- To light a flame of belief in yourself so strong that it becomes a magnificent obsession in your daily trading routine

- To cease procrastination in journaling and planning as the habits of successful trading are seared into your system

What differentiates the successful achiever from the wishful thinker? The inner strength gained from a religious observance of specific rules and a detailed goal and vision that makes your heart sing and your passion soar with an unshakable belief in yourself—even in the face of draw downs. Some have suggested that it is possible to take emotion out of the trading equation. Well, that is nearly impossible, simply because humans are emotional beings. It is possible to become detached to a degree and develop the emotional distance that holds back fear, greed, doubt and worry, but the reality is that these emotions still raise their ugly head—and often. It is far more realistic and effective, therefore, to acknowledge our emotions and learn how to harness them, making those emotions our ally rather than our foe, learning to wield the power of positive emotions so that desire and passion work in your favor. It has been said that trading should be like making a sandwich—rote, automatic, and according to protocol. To a degree this is true. What is more the case is that your hunger prompted you to "want" that sandwich in the first place; and that hunger, or desire, will not be satisfied until you devour it. That same hunger can—and often does—turn into greed (one sandwich is not enough, two is not enough, and so on). Depending on how "hungry" we are, we might be able to put off making that sandwich, but once the hunger has reached its zenith, the beast must feed, and we begin our process to create what we want. In fact, throughout the process, we are salivating; we are focused, and we are consumed by our desire to have it. Greed is a subset of desire, the part of desire that has transgressed the threshold; in other words, it is desire that has become distorted. What was once a mind-focusing emotion has become a mind-mangling problem. When we can separate supportive emotions from debilitating emotions, we can then tap into reservoirs of creative and compelling resources that bring to bear on making a successful trade. The goal is to ignite a mindset predisposed to making a "high probability" entry and a profitable "exit," with all the follow-through that keeps trading profitable. This is a process that honors "reality," that respects what is in the chart. It is a process that supports your ability to become "at one with the market."

The market is an organic, undulating thing, animated by the decisions of living beings. Price action is driven by human behavior and, as such, it is a reflection of an organic process that represents the hopes, fears and aspirations of every trade that takes place. The psychology of trading is about becoming at one with this price action. And it's about using the mediating element of our minds to tap into the "market-mind," the collective consciousness of every tick and pulse of the market. By becoming at one with the market, we initiate the Zen of market analysis.

Many books and workshops have included some very important aspects of the psychology of trading by encouraging habits such as:

- Developing and following a plan

- Creating and following a set of trading rules

- Maintaining discipline

- Identifying and using the right position sizing for your portfolio

- Choosing a strategy that fits with your temperament and personality
  Incorporating the discipline to follow through

Although important, providing these points to an individual uneducated in the psychology of trading is like telling him or her to fix a great dish without sharing the ingredients; handing him or her the keys to a car and not demonstrating how to drive or providing a map without sharing how to use it or imparting the importance of a compass.

Most businesses share common attributes. They include:

- Follow-through

- Self-confidence

- Self-investment

- Drive

- Knowledge

- Planning

- Organization

- Perseverance

- Creativity

From Pain to Profit has amassed a set of 'mind tools' that will:

- Help you plumb the depths of your inner strength

- Demonstrate how to compose the ingredients of successful trading

- Harness the power of your mind using passion and emotion as an ally
  Teach you how to avoid falling prey to it as a devouring beast

About the Author

Dr. M. Woodruff Johnson is the former Executive Director of the Kaiser Permanente Watts Counseling and Learning Center. Currently, he is President of Peak Performance 2000, Center for Human Potential, an organizational and personal development company. Dr. Johnson's doctorate is in Clinical Psychology and he holds two additional master degrees. He was also awarded a Coro Foundation Fellowship in Public Affairs and a Eureka Communities Fellowship. He holds certificates in Accelerated Learning, Neurosensory Development and hypnotherapy, among others. He has a passion for helping others to achieve their goals and get the results in life that they desire. He has provided clinical staff services in hospitals and community clinics as well. Dr. Johnson has been using mind/body healing techniques both professionally and personally with much success for many years. He actively trades Stock Options, Forex and Futures.

Acknowledgments

I want to acknowledge the support and assistance of many people that helped to make this book possible. My first interview was with Mike Mc Mahon, Director of Education at Online Trading Academy. His many years of successful trading and educating people just like me was instrumental in guiding my research. I am grateful for his contribution. Also there were a number of other instructors on the Online Trading Academy staff to whom I am grateful: Fernando Gonzalez, Gabe Velazquez, Brandon Wendel, CMT; Roger Best, and much thanks to JC Coldren, President of OTALA and Todd Davis General Manager of OTALA.

Trading is Psychological Warfare: We Have Seen the Enemy and It Is Us

"To manage our lives and our time more effectively, we need to replace the 'clock' with a 'compass'--because where we're headed is more important than how fast we're going." - Stephen Covey

Because you're reading this book, chances are you have felt the pain and anguish associated with getting results that you don't want... enough anguish that you are willing to try something different. You've lost money; you've seen apparently perfect trades blow up in your face repeatedly; and you have watched your portfolios shrink like saran wrap on a hot stove. Well, you've come to the right place. Trading is not for emotional dummies; it is psychological warfare. You may think that forces in the market are against you and that you are doing battle with other traders. To some extent that is true. Trading is a zero sum game, and for every winner, there is a loser. Every year, hundreds, perhaps thousands, of traders fall by the wayside because smart traders have taken their money—in some cases all of their money. But don't be mistaken. Those smart traders are not the ones you should be wary of first, for in the words of Pogo the cartoon figure, "We have seen the enemy and it is us." First you must do battle with, and overcome your biggest enemy... You. That's why trading is psychological warfare.

Trading in the financial markets is not rocket science, and the mechanics of trading can be quite easy—that is, if you're a computer. For humans who harbor normal emotional development in the context of culture, trading in the financial markets is arguably the single most challenging business venture upon which one can embark. Not because it offers the possibility of large gains and, therefore, large losses. This risk/reward element can be found in most entrepreneurial pursuits or corporate endeavors. No, what separates trading from other business forms is that each moment of choice, each decision point in the trade, involves immediate gain or loss and, therefore, tacit pleasure or pain. This prospect—for most people—ignites either fear or greed, depending on which side of the order you're on. And why such an extreme case of emotions? The answer, simply, is because we're talking about money.

Since the 16th century, the western world has been culturally predicated upon capitalism. Our way of life is inextricably tied to an economic social system driven by the marketplace. The language we use is infused with our economic orientation. We talk about economies of scale and the marketplace of ideas. Capital is king in our world, especially in the USA, to the extent that any idea or movement even remotely resembling what capitalists feel is socialist or—heaven forbid—communist, and branded as evil. Success is defined by the amount of money and materials one has. Power and influence are direct derivatives of capital, and even our august governmental bodies have been susceptible to the influence and corruption of money. And, on the personal level, when dealing with the financial markets, money is tied up in our definitions of self; money has a direct relationship to whether or not we feel powerful, competent, smart, and/or attractive, or, on the other hand, emasculated, ineffective, undesirable and/or stupid.

When money is thrown into the equation, the 'cool factor' becomes skewed because, in our minds, the stakes have become very high. Every weakness, blemish and character flaw in your personality will be challenged, called out and punked while trading in the financial markets. And it's not just about winning or losing. If that were the case, the game would not be so dire. Most of us have grown up with competition in one form or another; competition that we've more or less come to accept. We all know that with competition, there are winners and losers, but this element of money is tied into deep-seated fantasies and concepts that are as melodramatic sounding as life and death. Even on the surface, the notion of survival is acute, financial and otherwise, and it looms on our conscious horizon like a bad storm moving ever closer. In fact, the trading highways and byways are strewn with the dried bones of those who blew up accounts, suffered embattled business relationships and mangled marriages. And some of them lost everything, including their self-respect.

And now that I've established that trading is psychological warfare, I'd like to seemingly contradict myself. We actually don't want to do battle with ourselves. We do want to garner control, but not through mental violence. The reason for the war metaphor is that some people relate to it as a seriousness indicator. Yes, it is of grave importance to harness impulsive and compulsive behavior. It is, however, more important and arguably more effective to make an ally of our errant predilections. In other words, we want to become congruent and aligned in our intentions and emotions, because emotions are irrevocably part of our makeup. Also, those emotions that cause system distress and erratic behavioral disruptions have their origins in unconscious defensive structures developed in early-learned limitations. These learned limitations have their origins in the wounds we suffered at the hands of our family, loved ones, and authority figures. As a way to mitigate the emotional pain and protect against future wounding, parts of our younger self initiated a defense pattern to ward off potentially harmful demons. These parts of our "self" created a mythology—a story if you will—about the event or events that originally caused the pain. These events might be about love, friendship, loyalty, food, play, sex, money or anything. So, you see, our "selves" are attempting, through often-counterproductive measures, to come to our aid, and the most powerful way to address these "parts" is to engage them and entreat them to identify other creative ways to address the issues from which they want to protect us . One of the ways to do this is called 'reframing'. We will discuss this in more detail in later chapters.

Trading is a tough row to hoe for the faint hearted, the risk-averse, or the undisciplined. In fact, trading books are replete with advice pointing out the need for discipline, but few offer a way out of the forest of impulsive and compulsive actions, the behavioral seedlings of fear and greed and the impetus for discipline's necessity. Once those emotions grip us, our perceptions distort, our thinking clouds, and our judgment is impaired. We stop seeing reality as it is, and instead are seduced by impetuous illusions stemming from our misguided perceptions.

The Need for Self-Discipline

I've heard so many trading instructors mention the importance of self-discipline; and it's true, you will not make it as a professional trader if you cannot exercise discipline. If you can't make and keep commitments to yourself, you face a major challenge. Success requires a trading plan that outlines the strategies you intend to employ, and the goals for:

- How you will trade

- What time of day you will trade

- How many trades you will make

- Your objectives for the amount of money you expect to make

Next, you need a set of rules to govern your trading: the entries and exits, what type of setups will do and won't, etc., and these rules all stem, in large part, from your trading plan.

And lastly, position sizing and money management are of paramount importance. Good money management will keep you in the game even in the face of massive draw downs.

These are all critical elements of successful trading, but instructors in most cases only talk about the 'what' and not the 'how' of self-disciplined trading. This book is about developing the self-discipline necessary to overcome fear and greed, and in the process, become a highly successful trader.

In the words of Larry Wilson, author of *Play to Win*, it all starts with whether your orientation to life is a *play to win* strategy or one of *playing not to lose*. Allow me to explain. A *playing not to lose* strategy or philosophical orientation is based on the need to remain in the zone of comfort and convenience. Since we generally feel threatened and fearful, we are constantly looking for emotional relief. Things must come easily and without diligence when playing not to lose. People with this strategy are constantly looking for the magic bullet or the quick fix that will create results out of thin air with no regard for their creation. In other words, the glass is half empty. The philosophy of playing to win, on the hand, is steeped in the notions that:

- Life is growth
- Courage and challenge are harbingers of success
- Life is infinitely abundant
- Trust, commitment to excellence, and learning are paramount for professional and personal effectiveness

The core maps (our mental models or paradigms that filter perceptions) of *playing not to lose* are scarcity and distrust. An individual with a playing not to lose outlook might say to themselves, "I *must* make this trade because I can't possibly allow any trades to slip by; that is money lost, so I've got to do it now." Conversely, the person who plays to win knows that there is an abundance of opportunities, that one does not have to chase every trade impulsively because there will always be another, and another after that – she knows that there is power in stopping. Playing to win also entails the search for objective reality and absorbing it, holding on to it as you would a life jacket in a stormy sea. A *playing not to lose* strategy is closed with limited alternatives that constrict creativity; it blames others or outside influences first and seldom looks inside to identify salient issues that negatively affect results. It is irrational. The *play to win* strategy holds the "self" accountable and owns all results seeking to identify through various techniques, like journaling what is not working in order to effect changes in the system. The person using this approach is prepared to incorporate sound systems, protocols and effective routines to ensure sustainable success. This strategy is intellectually and emotionally honest and garners the enthusiasm and energy necessary to vigorously improve your investment strategy. *Playing not to lose* encourages erratic and illogical behaviors while looking for the easy win; it often puts large positions at risk, thereby simply gambling, and by reneging on commitments to their established rules—if they have rules at all. The *play to win* strategy recognizes that trading necessitates losses and that effective long-term winning means managing risk, having an iron clad commitment to the rules, goal-setting, planning and methodical, smart trading. The *play to win* or "trade-to-win" strategy is winning the psychological war one battle at a time and going as far as one can in a growth oriented, fun, honest and healthy way; otherwise it is simply "trading-not-to-lose."

The Attitude – The Springboard for Passion

One of the great myths today is that very successful traders somehow have never made or don't make mistakes, or that they win because they have enormous amounts of luck. Sound familiar? The fact is that, as humans, everybody makes mistakes, and some of the super achievers and market wizards at points in their lives seemed to make it a "past-time." No matter what heights great achievers rise to, they all have made many, and sometimes devastating, mistakes along the way. Mohammed Ali, possibly the greatest boxer of all time, made a number of tactical errors in some of his fights and lost as a result. Michael Jordan has missed countless free throws, many easy shots, and other mistakes while arguably becoming one of the greatest basketball players in history. And if these guys have a rocky time of it, just think of the obstacles normal people like you and I have to contend with.

One of the reasons we make mistakes, aside from being human, is that we are easily distracted by emotions. Like phantom hands, emotions grab our throats, and before we know what's happening, we choke. How many times have you been in a trade and your rule might state, "I do not chase trades!" But, as you look at that Maribuzo or blast-off, long, green candle, suddenly you are struck by the notion, "Man, I have to jump on this trade. It has money written all over it!" And then, unfortunately, you buy the high of the day at a strong resistance level and watch it plummet, taking with it any optimism for profit on that trade. Afterwards, you say to yourself, "What was I thinking? Now, I've lost again. I did exactly what I said I would not do."

How does it make you feel? What is it that helps the wizards maintain focus at these critical times? It is an unmitigated commitment to focus on their rules. These rules, along with other critical cogs in their trading machinery, are the religion of their business. They are passionate first about doing what it takes to be consistently successful; they abhor gambling in the markets and consider winning to be an equation that honors keeping commitments first. They define success in the markets as a function of percentages over an extended period of time, not by how much money is made in the short term. They develop and nurture a powerful desire to follow the successful protocol for getting the results that they want. When you want something with an intense desire, the true nature of your potential is realized through the fire in your passion. Conventional wisdom states that if you really want to do something with enough fervor, you'll do it, right? It is just a matter of finding and living the passion.

Another myth we dispel is one associated with self-discipline. To most people, self-discipline has to do with saying, "I'm gonna make myself do it," or with having willpower, or biting the bullet. Does this sound familiar? Well, the problem lies in the fact that these notions about self-discipline tax the system enormously and often lead to stress, burnout, or something even more pernicious-- psychosomatic illness. With psychosomatic illness, the ailment is real—ulcers, severe headaches, backaches, depression or major fatigue—but the cause can't be found. Obviously, this type of self-discipline is on par with the successful operation that kills the patient—the cure is worse than the ailment.

Identifying and accessing passion most often releases a chain reaction, a magnificent obsession, that rages deep inside. This is the self-discipline of being internally driven and attracting into your life that which makes your heart sing. And when you find joy in what you do, you are going 'to play' instead of 'to work'. This kind of desire overwhelms fear, doubt, greed and worry in its flames. There is little room or energy for disruptive emotions or for anything to stand between you and your desired results. You simply must have it. Also, with passion, your focus is razor sharp and your attention to detail rises. You find yourself thinking about it all the time. Do you remember when you first fell in love? You thought about every detail, you didn't want to miss anything, and you thought about her or him all the time. This emotional fixation tunes the body, mind, and spirit to work similarly for anything it focuses on. It brings the intuition, creativity, and spontaneity of the subconscious mind to bear on the desired object. As the saying goes, you become "hungry." You "want it so bad you can taste it." You "feel it in your bones" and "see" the outcome through a mental picture that keeps your drive alive. There is a good reason why these sayings revolve around sensations. The mental image gives focus to the heartfelt dream by providing specifics, like sounds, sights, smells and tastes, making the whole brain come alive with desire. The subconscious is then working as hard for the goal as the conscious is. And it makes much of the accomplishment seem easy and effortless—it just seems to happen. In other words, self-discipline sets a roadmap or blueprint in the subconscious to achieve the desire. The roadmap or blueprint to attracting what brings you inner joy involves and includes what is necessary to achieve it, and in the case of trading, rules and money management are woven into the fabric of consistent winning trades. And we know that the brain is only as strong as its weakest 'think'!

Going further, this kind of emotional passion or self-discipline also is purposeful and oriented to the objective. It has a feedback system so that, as reality changes, the goal is modified to fit. After each goal is achieved, a new course is set for achievement. The template changes as requirements change.

Actually, this concept of self-discipline is age-old. Our human system is a wondrous creation of which we are using only about 3%. In fact, Karl Pribram—thought by many to be the father of neuroscience—has supported Clement Steven's quote, "What the brain of man can conceive, his mind will achieve." Of his many contributions and thoughts, there are two that I particularly like:

1) The brain forms images and is governed by images of achievement, and the body cannot mobilize without them. Also, the development of an iron will is forged in the fire of emotion.

2) Neural blueprints are made by both physical and emotional images. This is also the basis for such books as Think and Grow Rich by Napoleon Hill, and Psycho-Cybernetics by Dr. Maxwell Maltz.

When we imagine, (either positively or negatively) our brain can't tell the difference, and through the release of neurotransmitters and hormones in the brain, we either feel good or bad with the vision or thought. This is a gross oversimplification, but I trust that you "get the picture." So, the more we want that new car or that house on the ocean or that dream vacation—and the more we can see, hear, touch, taste and smell it in our imagination—the more real the brain treats it. The more passion and emotion that is generated, especially when coupled with a specific vision, the closer we come to getting it. But, there is a catch: if I gave you the combination to a safe containing a million dollars in it, you'd feel pretty excited about the prospects of opening the safe. Right? That is until you realized that the 10-digit number was not in sequence and you really didn't have the combination. Therefore, self-disciplined trading involves the correct sequence and combination of behaviors in order for the subconscious mind to work for you rather than against you. And you know how it can work against you. How many times have you slapped your forehead and thought, "What was I thinking when I entered that trade?" or "Why did I do that?" or, "Darn, I told myself that I was going to do it according the plan that I set for myself, and I screwed it up again by not following through."

The subconscious is powerful; it can make you sick, and it can heal you. What I want to do is show you how to do is harness that power.

So, peak performance trading bridges the gap between wishful thinking and the trading results you want. The most powerful tool you have is right between your ears, as long as you learn the combination to unlock your inner self and unleash this strength.

Consider a child just learning about her world. Does she need to be told to listen, to look, to imitate, to try and try again? A child is driven, and if she sees what she wants, she's got to have it, or if she sees behavior, she must imitate. She struggles, falls and rises, as she is obsessed with learning to walk. She makes sounds and tries to talk with a dogged determination.

That baby is keyed into a passion that drives her to see, to listen, to imitate, and to learn. The passion that drove you as a baby is still inside you; it is a part of your humanness. Unfortunately, we are also taught to remove ourselves from the passion as we become socialized into "good citizens." Socialization can stifle curiosity, creativity and that playful spirit that sees life as a series of games and puzzles to figure out. When this happens, or when we become "grown up," that inner spark to explore the reasons why, and to be wide-eyed at the wonders of life, is often lost to the detriment of a rich and growth-oriented life. But, when rekindled, this passion galvanizes our energy, curiosity and trial-and-error courage.

Making mistakes in the service of learning becomes a way of life. This passionate attunement to doing what effectively magnetizes your desires to you also makes you feel like a hungry lion just out of captivity, driven by the deep desire to do that which gets you the results you want. Consider the prey the lion must stalk and kill in order to survive and thrive; if she does not learn to do that effectively and in the proper sequence, she will not eat and surely will perish. She must learn the process of hunting first in order to be successful in the hunt.

Using this metaphor, the protocol of steps involved in successful trading is stalking, patiently waiting, identifying the high probability target, and then entering the pursuit. You first want to ensure that you have that reality firmly locked in your mind. You must develop the intense desire to learn the hunt, or to do whatever it takes to ensure success, and get that prey.

Motivation is also part and parcel to this conversation. We are not speaking of external motivation, the kind you get from listening to a rousing speech or a riveting trading lecture. This is an *outside* source. This is a good starting place, but it doesn't last. It has artificial peaks. The day after the speech, you're 30 minutes early to your trading desk, doing homework and vowing that you're going to "do it right." This may last just long enough for the trade to go against you—then, with one failure to include a stop loss, you're back in the same boat, and the rules might as well be thrown overboard. This kind of motivation leaves you with a false sense of well-being. You get a shot in the arm, but it wears off.

Then there is the most obvious "fool's gold" motivation—money. It too is short lived, because money is transient and of itself has no substance; it is only good as a medium of exchange. You can't eat it, drink it, live in it, drive it or wear it, at least not for very long. Many believe that they want money, but to be specific, what they really want is what money can buy. I would contend that if you had everything that you have ever desired, money would lose all of its appeal.

Another word for money is greed. It distorts reality into a phantom of itself, resulting in decisions based on conjured notions of what we "think" will happen, not what is taking place in the charts. Thus, money as a motivator is a poor prospect.

Then, there is fear: "if I don't succeed in this trade then I am screwed!" Fear, like greed, fragments, blurs and moves you to grasp for fading phantoms that leave you as bait in waters teeming with sharks eager to feed on your capital. I'm sure you've heard the adage: "Scared money does not win." The only motivation that moves you to identify what is required for consistent long-term results is that which is forged in the heart space of your inner self where those results are tied to reasons like family security, a richness of life, personal pride in doing a good job, and/or peer recognition. This is where your passion resides.

10 Characteristics of Highly Successful People

Let's take a look at the 10 characteristics of high-achieving wizards.

1. A Strong Sense of Purpose

The first winning characteristic is the ability to develop a strong sense of purpose. The consistent winner identifies what she wants and then pursues it, despite all the negatives. This is the real reason for making the effort, and it is well defined. The undisciplined person doesn't know what they want; they often have no direction, can't make a decision, are consistently changing, constantly looking outside themselves for the answer, and are forever starting projects they never finish.

2. Goal Setting

The third characteristic relates to goal setting and creating a sensory-rich vision. The undisciplined have vague goals that they might *maybe* someday achieve. They are capable of sensory-rich images but apply it to doom-and-gloom scenarios, such as coming up with a long list of reasons and ways that the trade will not work out. Achievers visualize their outcomes clearly and creatively, using all their senses to taste, see, hear, touch and smell the goal. They also feel the tingling and ecstatic rush of what it will feel like before it ever happens. They create the emotion of winning, which takes the spark of purpose and turns it into a flame—from *I think I can* to a heartfelt *I know I can.*

3. A Positive Sensory Orientation

The forth characteristic is that achievers have a positive sensory orientation. They expect to succeed. They see past accomplishments, no matter how small, as proof of the pudding—they did it before and can do it again. They are not afraid of risks and trying new approaches. They never lose site of the goal, and they *never* admit defeat. Each failure is a new and valued lesson that takes them

---

closer to their goal. The undisciplined waste their time dwelling on past failures, reinforcing their belief that there is no reason to keep trying. They develop a fear of failure, and this attitude becomes a self-fulfilling prophesy of failure generating failure.

4. A Role Model or Mentor

The second characteristic of the self-disciplined achiever is that they have aligned themselves with a role model and/or a mentor, someone whose advice they trust. In fact, when a man asks you for advice, you can figure he isn't married!! Throughout history, great men and women have looked to role models for inspiration, guidance and motivation to succeed. And with good reason: Why reinvent the wheel? The achiever studies the life pattern of the successful person, someone who is already achieving what she desires. The undisciplined look for the quick-fix models; they think it's a gimmick, that it's luck, or who you know. These people resent the truly successful. They can't admit that intense success takes intense focus and perseverance to succeed. They blame their lack of success on excuses; bad breaks, bad luck, and/or bad parents, and see themselves as victims.

5. Self-Assuredness

The fifth characteristic is self-assuredness, which the last four characteristics help develop. Heavy rollers are fueled by self-confidence. They have a strong, gut-level belief in self and their ability, which is unshakeable. Deep down in their heart, they know that they can do it. The undisciplined are hampered by self-doubt. The foreboding of failure haunts them and fills their mind with fear and stifles their ability to take risks. They end up slamming the door on their own possibilities.

6. The Ability to Plan and Organize

Next is the ability to plan and organize. The undisciplined have no clear game plan. Their attention is scattered. The skill of prioritizing eludes them and they make endless lists of tasks that never get done. They are disorganized and waste time and energy chasing illusions of what they think they want. Or they have too many irons in the fire and can't keep track of them. Achievers break goals into pieces and work with one job at a time. They are methodical. They prioritize their time and accomplish first things first. Without planning and organization, even the most brilliant idea has no value.

7. The Necessary Education

Heavy-hitting wizards acquire the knowledge necessary to make the game plan work. The undisciplined look for short cuts. They take a weekend course and are suddenly 'experts' or listen to one person's advice and think they know it all. To them, it is too much trouble to get it right; they lack patience. They don't want to put the time in to discover the crucial details and always get sidetracked into doing something else. Winners identify the necessary knowledge and acquire it, going back to school if necessary. They recognize the critical importance of learning how to do it right the first time.

8. Patience

The eighth characteristic of peak performance is patience. The undisciplined want everything now and can't wait. They view time as the enemy and think it will be wasted if they don't get on it right now, without the proper preparation, like starting a trading business without a business plan or entering a trade without a trading plan. All real achievers possess patience. They understand that true accomplishment takes time. Time does not intimidate this achiever; in fact, time becomes immaterial. It becomes a tool. They know, as they are working on the goal, that each passing minute takes them closer to its achievement. When engrossed in their passion, they become immersed and the goal becomes everything. Also, achievers enjoy the *process*. It is exciting and getting there is at least half the fun.

9.   Persistence and Perseverance

Next in the lineup of success traits are persistence and perseverance. The undisciplined are driven by quick fixes and impulsive schemes, and they are at the mercy of greed and fear. As soon as the tick goes against them, they panic, and their minds are no longer focused on what the charts are giving. They see only what the distortion will allow. They are easy quitters when the going gets tough. They only dream and never create the steam. They are always complaining about the market or their losses but never do anything about it. Big time achievers stick to their vision despite setbacks. They don't give up when met with hardships or the negative opinions of others. Successful achievers are relentless and stubborn. They succeed against all odds, and when they are discouraged, they draw inspiration and motivation from their sensory-rich vision.

10. The Ability to Experience Pleasure

Self-disciplined achievers have the ability to experience pleasure while working on their vision. The undisciplined are workaholics and often experience stress, pain and boredom while working. They *tolerate* work between periods of partying. Many live for the weekend and make money to have fun. Real achievers do what makes their heart sing. They can't believe they are getting paid to have so much fun. They are engrossed in their work, and excited by their goals. It is easy for them to work on their vision because their vision is their passion, their pleasure.

The 7 Secrets of Self-Disciplined Trading: Self-Mastery is a Quality of Kings

"Be vigilant in your control over the self. If you cannot respond to your will, how can you expect others to respond? - From The Way of Kings

This program involves an integrated *sequence* of steps. I emphasize sequence because many traders and other business owners suffer from a very insidious disease that could be called "outofsequencialism," that is, being out of sequence in your business, your life, and, more importantly, your way of thinking. This is a very important point. Life, living and everything life has to offer are replete with examples of the absolute necessity for having the proper sequence.

Nature itself is all about sequencing. You could call it Nature's Law because everything follows a specific pattern, and it things must be in a specific order to ensure the desired results. How does a baby learn to walk? Babies begin by attempting to roll over. When the child is strong enough, it props itself up. Then the baby crawls, and afterwards stands, and begins to walk with assistance (around coffee tables, couches, etc.). Then finally your baby walks on his or her own. That is the *sequence* nature has given us, and eventually, we all walk on two feet.

Everything has a sequence, a specific set of steps that must be followed in a specific order, or it just doesn't work. Getting dressed, tying your shoes and driving your car are just a few illustrations. For example, driving your car involves a specific sequence:

1) Open the car door

2) Sit in the car

3) Engage the seat belt

4) Put the key into the ignition

5) Turn the key

6) Put your foot on the brake

7) Put the car in drive

8) Push the gas pedal

9) Navigate

This is a simple, uncomplicated sequence of activities you've performed thousands of times without really thinking about it, but in order to drive effectively, these steps must be performed in an ordered sequence. Think about this sequence for a moment. Can you put any of these steps out of order and get the results called 'driving your car'?

You might be asking yourself what this has to do with your trading business. There is a big chance that right now your trading business is dramatically out of sequence and you don't even realize it. You may be wondering why this approach doesn't work, and that the strategy you are using doesn't work. Well, if you are out of sequence, then you will not get your desired results.

These Seven Steps to Success have been formulated from the 10 characteristics of self-disciplined achievers. These steps employ the sub-conscious so that it works for you rather than against you. This avoids self-defeating behavior that for many begins with the inability to make and keep commitments. How often have you made a promise to yourself—like losing weight, starting to exercise, or learning a new skill—only to be frustrated because you never got beyond *wishing?* With the secrets of peak performance trading, the gap is bridged between wishful thinking and performing the sequence of actions that create consistent trading success. Wishful thinking is unengaged and does not actively sensualize the objective, thereby failing to harness the power of your mental and emotional turbines. Wishful thinking is a passive process that is energy deficient. It would be as ineffective as trying to satisfy the electrical needs of a city with the output of a household generator. As one learns the combination that will unleash the strength of the unconscious, the possibilities become infinite. Peak Performance Trading is a way to unlock this horizon of potential through using proven mind honing and power activating psycho-neuro techniques that tap motivation in the only place that it lasts—from within.

Let's look at the actual steps the make this process work:

Step 1: Develop a Strong Sense of Purpose

Many people continually ask, "How can I choose a life or trading path from so many choices?" In order to answer this question, we need to first find our reason for living and trading; getting to the main idea. Macro (large) and Micro (small) purposes change as we grow and develop. They can be applied to any goal, large or small. Finding your purpose is a logical and creative process. With purpose, goals become rational and easy to achieve. For example, if you were stranded in the wilderness during winter with no prospect of rescue or cover until the next day, your *macro purpose* would be to figure out how to stay alive. You would have several micro purposes: figuring out how to stay warm, make a fire, and so forth. If all of the micro purposes are achieved, then the macro- survival- is achieved. Another example is attending undergraduate school to achieve a BA degree. All the required classes are micro purposes that lead to the ultimate goal of a degree. If, however, we are striving for an MD degree, getting a BA is a micro purpose along with internships and several other requirements.

Your macro purpose for trading should point towards the direction that starts your journey to becoming a successful speculator. For example, to attain a wealthy lifestyle for you and your family, filled with travel, theater, music, fine dining and financially security, your micro purpose would be to identify the right financial market, whether stocks, futures, commodities or currencies, as well as to determine which avenue of success most resonates most with your personality and lifestyle.

Step 2: Create a Sensory Goal Statement

Once you have decided (from your limitless wishing and thinking—this can be found in the appendix) where your purpose can take you in terms of a goal, it is then time to make this goal clear and specific. There no doubt are many objectives and goals you would like to pursue. Take a moment and choose a goal from your purpose that is very important to you, and describe its details.

Step 3: Creating a Sensory-Rich Vision of Success

After your goal description is complete, you will use it to create your emotion-provoking vision of success in a 4-step process. When linked to success and mentor possibilities, this vision acts like a hot branding iron, burning deep into every fiber of your being. You will become obsessed with the vision and will develop a deep-seated belief in your ability to succeed, thus experiencing a quantum leap from a sense of possibilities to a sure-fire conviction: you will *know* you can do it.

Your vision of achievement is constructed first by using your purpose to provide concrete images. Photographs, books, magazines, and newspapers provide excellent illustrations of how people live your goal and vision.

First, Create a vision-achievement scrapbook and always be on the lookout for more pictures.

Second, list all the advantages and rewards you can think of that your goal will bring when achieved. Use photographs from your scrapbook to help and include results from your inner search. This furnishes desire, which motivates to positive action. In the inner search, see how your life will change, how it will affect your family and friends, and how *you* will change. Are you dressing differently? Are you involved in different activities? Are your friends different, and if so, how do they look? Do you live in a different place? If so what does it look like?

Thirdly, your vision should include the sights, sounds, touches, smells, tastes and emotions of all the benefits you can think of–scenes that put it all together. The more intense the vision, the more emotional power it will possess. Every time you conjure this vision, you will increase your drive and sustaining power, which will help you develop plans and habits, and help you persist and persevere, help you achieve goals. When you are finished, write it down, making sure it is full of emotion and enough enthusiasm to evoke the passion of your heart.

Fourthly, record the finished product on a CD or other medium. Be sure to capture the enthusiasm. Be very rich in description—the more specific, the more powerful, and the more it will help you reach your goals day after day, week after week, and month after month. Repeat this process until you are convincing in every detail. You may change this recording whenever new changes in your life occur, or if you decide to modify your vision with new and powerful images. The more you do this, the more vivid and powerful your vision it will become.

Four guidelines will help implant the goal in your mind and heart:

1) First thing each morning, review your purpose, goal statement, pictures of achievement and vision. This process will continually remind you of why you NEED to succeed. Part of this process will be achieved as you listen to your CD.

2) During the day, imagine your vision as much as possible, recalling every detail about the wonderful gains. Make a copy for the car and be liberal with the number of times that you listen.

3) At the end of the day, review those events that took you closer to your goal, no matter how small. A trip around the world begins with one step, and they may be baby steps. What is important is that you are moving, and consistent movement will get you there well before you know it.

4) Listen to your vision before going to bed. This refuels and reinforces the goal by providing daily feedback. Setbacks will occur and there may be times when adjusting the course is necessary. Remember, there is no effortless path, so change your vision to keep step with your reality.

Your sensory rich goal description encompasses the desire in a clear, concrete way. This vision fans the embers of conviction, causing emotions to flare and inciting the system to action. You leap from the possibilities of *I think I can* to the heartfelt, *I know I can.* This vision becomes your story of achievement, your flame of emotion that provides energy, creative power, and the desire to single-mindedly see the vision through to successful completion. The root word of emotion is motion—to move-- moving along a path unyielding and oblivious to distraction.

Step 4: Acquire a Role Model or a Mentor

The term mentor originates in Greek mythology with Odysseus and his travels. In his absence, he left a wise old man—his name was Mentor--to look after the kingdom. Mentor did such a fine job that his name became associated with wisdom and guidance.

All of our lives, we are influenced by role models, some negative and some positive. The difference between role models and mentors is that a role model can be from history or from the present, from fact or fiction, and your choice of role model sets an example using behavior and a pattern. Mentors, on the other hand, are actually available and provide guidance and interaction; a relationship may be fostered with them. You gain the power of possibilities by identifying with your role model. Once you learn about the role model, both strengths and weaknesses, they then become real and human. Nat King Cole, the great singer/piano player, had Errol Garner for a role model. Errol was a master piano player of his day who performed in Chicago clubs. Nat would sit by a club window in Chicago every evening when he was a teenager, studying Errol's riffs.

People with the same goals often think alike and usually have many similarities. William James once wrote: "… if you want a habit - act like you have it. The Central Nervous System can't distinguish from real experiences and strongly imagined ones. Acting as if has remarkable powers." Today, a common cliché is "Fake it 'til you make it." The only difference between you and great achievers is that they put forth a disciplined effort. With the same effort, you can achieve the same level of success. An Indian poem describes the old teacher of the children, "... and did you not see their faces when I called them warriors... Don't we become most quickly the person whom we think we are...? Inside they feel important so that someday they are important."

As you emulate your role model while working toward your goal, you are like a child playing dress up. Every time you imitate the successful behavior, it becomes more and more a part of you. Actors spend months studying a part before they play it, but when they know it, they are completely believable.

When first looking for role models and mentors, consult books, films and biographies with the understanding of your purpose. Ask yourself questions, such as:

- *What do I need to do?*
- *What do I need to learn?*
- *What actions do I need to take?*
- *Did the main character achieve what you had chosen?*

There are basically several methods of looking for and choosing a role model/mentor.

1. Family acquaintances or close family members. Pay close attention to how they solve problems and deal with challenges.

2. Networking

Network by participating in trading organizations, fraternities and sororities, social opportunities, and any event with individuals who might be interested in or are practicing what you have chosen as your purpose.

3. One powerful method is apprenticeship. Many high achievers have found apprenticeships where they can learn from a master in a close relationship, exposing them to all the details. In choosing an apprenticeship, you'll want to ask questions that give you a clear indication as to whether or not this person is good for you, including:

- How did they develop their knowledge and skills?
- Did they attend any special schools or read any special books?
- How many hours do they work per day?
- How do they handle pressure and stress?
- Do they love what they do?
- Do they have time for family and friends? A
- re they calm and in control?
- Do they listen well and make their own decisions?

Your mentor will have many faults; this is the nature of being human. Actually, mistakes bring the two of you closer by making your mentor 'real'. If imperfect people can do it, so can you. Most undisputed great artists and performers still become jittery and anxious when confronted with their idol, even though they may have surpassed them in achievement.

Most achievers draw inspiration and strategy from role models and mentors. As the story of the role model and mentor unfolds, a pattern begins to form: the role model's thinking, style and action can be emulated. By following this pattern you can begin to rate your own strengths and weaknesses. You must learn what you don't know first, both about you and about what is necessary to trade successfully. With time, you begin to use this deeper self-understanding a part of your own personality. You develop an emotional belief that you can do it, just like your mentor did. That tiny spark, with proper nurturing, becomes an ember, and then a bonfire

Remember:

a) Make it time specific, so that it may be supported by planning and organizing.

b) It must be results oriented, focusing attention on what you want.

c) It should be measurable, with criterion for completion, so that the progress may be tracked. Also, this provides motivation every time a micro goal is met, fueling your drive to work consistently and systematically.

Here is a good example of how you might commit your goals on paper: Purpose:

I want financial security for my family. I want to put all of my children through college

Goal: by Dec 2009, I will have enrolled in and completed an options trading course and will be trading live money.

Step 5: Develop Organization and Planning

Planning is the first action inspired by emotion. Here you will identify and formulate a sequence of steps, a routine or protocol that will make your vision a reality. On a macro level, we are talking about organizing and planning your trading business; on a micro level, it is about organizing your trading session and planning your trades. Your focus is to figure out how to accomplish the goal and what actions it will require. This process turns your vision into a concrete goal, further fueling the fires of emotion and action. Additionally, it is important to organize both on a macro level and a micro level in order to plan effectively.

The German philosopher Johan Wolfgang Van Gerta once said: "What you can do or dream, begin it, boldness has genius power and magic..." Here is where the vision is brought to life and turned into a practical process, a step-by-step action plan. Dreams are a dime a dozen. Everybody has them. But it is their execution that is most important.

This plan, then, is a logical map showing where you want to go and how you will get there. "When a man doesn't know what harbor he is headed for, no wind is the right one." Ideas take concentrated work. Concentrated work involves details. Too many people think that others should do the detailed work. They delegate research, back-testing and homework to others. You've seen the person who consistently looks for "tips" or wants someone to "tell" them what or where the good trade is. When this happens, you can't blame anyone but yourself if things go wrong. The person in charge must attend to details, and that person is you, the trader; in fact, if the details are ignored, the trading plan is likely to fail. But the devil is in the details, potentially causing one to drown in the myriad of miniscule minutia. It is hard and can be monotonous, but research, back testing, and paying attention to technical analysis details must be done.

Planning is a way to look at the whole and the parts that make up the whole. It is a way to look at the parts logically and sequentially. One step should lead to another. In other words, each step taken makes the next step possible, like studs in a railroad track. This pertains to both large (macro) and small (micro) activities.

Successfully following the plan increases self-confidence and pride. When this is realized, you are on your way to being a self-disciplined achiever, a peak performance trader. Every small accomplishment is living proof that it can be done. Every step closer to the goal reinforces and expands your faith in the accomplishment of the goal and supports your ability to make decisions.

Of course, ideas take time to implement. For example, many successful traders share that it takes 2-3 years to become a proficient, successful speculator.

Don't forget the micro goals and macro goals as you move along on your journey. The big picture is very important when considering tasks with many steps. Building a house is a good example. The micro goals might be to:

1) Level the site

2) Build the foundation

3) Pour the foundation

4) Frame the structure

5) Wire the house

6) Lay the plumbing

7) Build the roof

The time spent on these micro goals may take weeks, months or years. You must develop patience with a sense of time on your side to assure the goal. In order to meet short and long-range goals, it is important to organize resources and create schedules. This helps focus direction and organize wherewithal. Every moment of planning saves 3 or 4 in execution. It is logical and easy to visualize steps and apply them to both your Business Plan and to your Trading Plan.

There are four basic components of the planning process:

1) Look at the big picture to allow the subconscious system, or right brain, to size it up intuitively.

2) Take time to complete each step before moving on to the next; otherwise it's like driving and starting your turn before you get to the intersection. You are bound to cause an accident.

3) Pay attention to the details.

4) Remember that planning and implementation is a trial and error process. You will make mistakes. Some are unavoidable.

A note about mistakes: Mistakes are nothing more than springboards to learn and build capacity. When you make a mistake, include in your journal what you saw and what was your plan. Afterwards, print the chart so that you will have a visual account of what the trade looked like so you can etch what to look for the next time the chart price action appears again. You learn from it and consequently can avoid repeating it. Remember, experts make big mistakes but turn them into successes. When Coca Cola introduced a new coke product and discontinued the original Coke, there was such an outcry that they brought it back under the name Classic Coke, and to this day have a bigger market share. They are stronger that ever, and the "mistake" helped them to make more money.

Using your mistakes from the planning process creates self-directing behavior. This is called "Cybernetics." This was NASA's planning tool. In 1960, President Kennedy gave the United States a directive to put a man on the moon by 1970; it was accomplished by 1969. NASA took the objective "put a man on the moon," and broke it down into micro objectives. When the project started, they made a flow chart of what they had to do. For instance, they had to build a new rocket that would stay in orbit around the planet for longer and longer periods of time. Space suits had to be designed. Each step brought them closer and closer to the objective until the job was completed.

NASA, with the help of flow charts, created a Visual Network Plan in order to achieve the goal of a man in space. It was visual because they could look at the components and identify and visualize the steps necessary. It was a network because each step connected in a logical system showing how the different parts lead to the goal. Moreover, it was a living, working system.

The following phases can be used to designing a visual network plan:

- Write down the target as a way of representing the whole of it conceptually.

- Break the target into major steps or activities.

- Organize the steps into a logical order.

- Design a visual network of each activity (to get another picture that is more defined).

- Estimate the time necessary for each activity to be completed.

- Set calendar dates to each activity.

- Work up a number of versions before you finalize the plan.

After you design your visual network plan, write a story of your achievement. This story will contain all that you did to hit the target. Write in the past tense. It should include elements such as:

- How long did it take to reach the goal?

- What did each step feel like along the way?

- Was the goal reevaluated as the plan unfolded?

- What did you discover about yourself?

Be sure to brag as you relay how you attacked and conquered each activity exhibiting plenty of enthusiasm. Make sure the story rings true in your mind and heart. Additionally, you'll want to keep it simple, as though you were telling a friend. After the plan is written, read it to yourself aloud. Take note if there are places that did not seem or feel true. These are indicators of places where you must continue to work on the vision.

Step 6: Educate Yourself to Make the Game Plan Work

In this "information-is-power" age, you need knowledge and skill to succeed at any goal. There is a tremendous amount of Fundamental Analysis and Technical Analysis minutia involved in successful equity, futures and currency trading. However, getting that knowledge can be a daunting task. Also, our attitude regarding our internal stories about our ability to learn and assimilate knowledge can be either a boon or a bane to the undertaking. Often, we become our own worst enemy due to those internal stories. For instance, we determine what we need to learn and to do; then we get the story about how difficult it's going to be, or how we "flubbed" it up the last time we tried it. This type of internal story is called a "negative feedback loop." In many cases a negative feedback loop can disrupt and dislodge one's ability to learn and stay on the learning course. Negative feedback loops most often are established in childhood and built upon the negative messages we received about ourselves from authority figures, family, and peers. These negative loops proceed very much like recorded messages that have been playing and replaying in our thoughts since very early ages—phrases like "You can't do that", "You'll never make it", "You dummy", "You'll never amount to anything", and other types of abuse. Statements like these are hurtful even as an adult, and may have left you with low self-esteem, a poor self-image and, in some cases, self-hatred. If you've swallowed these labels whole, they can't be digested by your system. They remain stuck, deep in the psyche, leaving you frozen at that point in your childhood development with the same logic and reasoning abilities of a child at that age. Consequently, you react automatically when the stifled part of your personality is activated by external circumstances or events pushing the button on your recorder. However, with self-knowledge and learning how to successfully handle the circumstantial triggers when they surface, your self-image is lifted, and the process of breaking the old negative loops is begun.

As an example, most people wouldn't try to run a marathon without the appropriate preparation; it's a foolish thing to attempt. If you really want to do it, you will greatly increase the probability of success if you builds up to it by running a little at a time, maybe a half-mile at first, then a mile, 3 miles, 5, then 10, 20, and so on. You also gain knowledge of how to train, and learn the importance of good nutrition. In other words, small steps create small but ever-increasing capacity and build self-confidence while building strength and know-how. With each new item learned, and with each win in a trading demo account, this activity serves to support the effort to take that small step and fuel the desire to take another.

A famous 1968 psychological study entitled "Pygmalion in the Classroom" by Robert Rosenthal and Lenore Jacobson, was done with two sets of children, one labeled "gifted" and the other labeled "slow" (only for purposes of the study). Those labeled as gifted were told that their potential was unlimited; those labeled as slow were left to their own devices. As you might imagine, even though the labeling was completely arbitrary, the 'gifted' children excelled, while the 'slow' children lived down to the expectations. Success breeds more success, no matter how small, and breaks negative loops with positive achievements.

An Approach to Learning New Skills and Abilities

Identify the skills and knowledge you need by asking, "Will I succeed without this skill or knowledge?" In this way, you will begin to develop the parameters of what you "need to know." This helps make the process logical and easy to follow with one step after the other, and prevents you from cluttering your mind with unnecessary information

After you have identified what you need to know, design a flow chart or mind map; that is a visual knowledge plan with a start box and a finish box, outlining things to learn at the same time in linear boxes (one under the other) and those that come one after another in horizontal boxes. For example, if you want to become a *medical doctor*, your visual knowledge network plan (that will be included in the overall visual network plan) gives you the strength to go on until you are finished by establishing the macro plan; that is, wanting to be a *neurosurgeon*, and the micro plan, *getting a BA with an A average in pre-med* and getting *guidance from an advisor and a role model - mentor*. In another example, if by asking questions you determine that you want to be an options trader, you would then identify what knowledge is necessary to become a successful options trader and from where this knowledge might be obtained. You would then chart out the visual network plan, with the first box being *stock trading* and subsequent boxes—like *fundamental analysis, basic technical analysis* and so on—moving toward the final box, an *options trader* (with boxes like *advanced technical analysis*, and *advanced options strategies*).

None of this is any use, however, unless you *believe* that you can learn. Negative belief loops established, false assumptions about subjects you may surely have the aptitude for, but not the attitude; things like math, etc., which you "just know" you can't learn. Why? Because that's the way it happened in school at a very early age. Einstein did poorly in elementary school and flunked college math; however, he had a dream and vision of what he wanted to do, which drove him to learn math in order to explain his vision to others. Dr. Mimen, the father of the laser and widely accepted as a genius, flunked his Ph.D. orals and had to retake them. Learning did not come easy for him.

Attitude is 90% of success. Rod Carew, the great former baseball player and coach, did not make his high school baseball team; his coach thought he wasn't good enough. But, through thousands of hours of practice, he became a professional player and went on to win 7 batting championships and became one of the few players who achieved over 3000 hits in his career. Don King, who as a youth wanted to become a lawyer, became a numbers bookmaker instead and went to prison for manslaughter. While in prison, he read literature and philosophy and made the decision to rehabilitate himself. Through correspondence courses, he maintained an A average at Ohio University and went on to promote charity boxing after his release. Soon after he convinced Mohammad Ali to put on a charity match in Cleveland, he became a promoter and manager grossing several hundred million dollars and building an empire of televised boxing events. Malcolm Forbes, of Forbes Magazine, did not make the staff of his college newspaper. Les Brown, the famous motivational speaker, was told he would never amount to much; that he was dumb. He knew what he wanted and learned how to make speeches. Little by little, he acquired new knowledge and skill, and today commands several thousand dollars for a one-hour speech, all paid in advance. With this same asset-based thinking, you can accomplish what you previously thought you could not because your belief in yourself has been raised. The negative feedback loop is broken through step-by-step accumulation of skills and knowledge.

The next thing to consider in this learning approach is Patience. Einstein once said: "...the more I learn, the more I realize I don't know, and the more I realize I don't know, the more I want to learn." Leaning new knowledge and skills is a systematic step-by-step process, acquiring knowledge fragment-by-fragment and building little by little on a cellular level. It necessarily takes time and starts off feeling very slow. Excellence is based on seasoned learning, sticking to it over a long period of time so that the brew has matured in its readiness and provides a full array of flavor and a distinctive style. The quick fix rarely works, bringing forth a very weak flavor and a flimsy style common in fluke situations, which can't weather the light of close scrutiny.

I am reminded of the young black welfare mother who had several children in her early twenties. Her life-long dream was to be an MD. This was a woman who had not graduated from high school. Can you imagine the ridicule and disbelief others had when she shared her dream and vision with them? But the passion for her desire was so strong that she began to take the baby steps necessary to get what she wanted, like getting her GED and beginning the process of going to college. Fueling her passion with visualization of her steps as she took class after class, getting A after A, success after success and weathering the failures along the way, eventually getting her BA and being accepted into medical school, graduating and doing her residency. She achieved her goal because she had a burning desire fueled by her vision of success, and her dogged determination would allow nothing or no one to come between her and that vision.

As you draw inspiration and fortitude from your vision, it doesn't matter how much or how hard it is to achieve. Every time you master a skill, your confidence in your ability to achieve increases. But to master a skill, you must first learn the necessary specifics of the game; you must acquire an intimate knowledge of not just what it takes, but what it is. To be skilled at chess, you must first learn the foundation of the game, how the game is played and what constitutes winning. Then you must learn exactly what skills are necessary. Next, you acquire each skill, and after that, you master each skill. When each skill has been learned and added to the toolbox, you become a master of the game. So it is with trading.

Because trading offers so many ways to participate, you must identify your trading temperament and disposition in order to uncover your profile. Armed with this knowledge, you can then identify what type of trading style and macro strategy best works with your personality; i.e., short term versus swing or long term, options versus buying stock, futures/commodities versus equities; forex vs. equities; day versus swing, and so forth.

Step 7: Persistence and Perseverance

One of the most important attributes leading to *self-disciplined success* is persistence and perseverance. Nothing worth having is captured and mastered overnight. It takes time and energy. You need to develop the dogged determination and the endurance to go the distance and become a winner. The drive to persist and persevere is fueled by the initial vision. The closer you get to the goal of process mastery, the stronger the belief and the clearer the vision, and the more real it becomes. As you continue this relationship and strive to achieve, the vision fuels the goal of process mastery and the goal of process mastery fuels the vision. With each tiny, private victory, you are developing more capacity for going to the next level of play. Like training for the marathon, it is achieved through a process of consistently building endurance and strength to go to the next level of achievement. Between the vision and the goal, this revolving course of action acts like a nuclear reactor and puts into motion a self-perpetuating spiral of vision, belief, emotion and reality. This self-perpetuating spiral will change your life from the inside out. This what motivates men and women to achieve greatness. Greatness is spawned by the development of an inner obsession with honoring commitments and consistent follow-through. Greatness lies in the understanding that it is not focusing on the win but mastering the fundamentals and consistent implementation that leads to the win. Greatness is in the grasp of each of us—you can program yourself for success with the right combination that unlocks the power of intention. Success is where opportunity meets preparation. Persistence here refers to the single-minded determination that each and every trade *must* follow all rules, the unyielding focus on habitually planning every single action in the markets, and the building of a greater and greater capacity for winning—and winning is defined as religiously keeping your commitments.

The Results Model: How Results Come About

"Until one is committed, there is hesitancy, the chance to draw back, always ineffectiveness. Concerning all acts of initiative and creation, there is one fact, one elementary truth, the ignorance of which kills countless ideas and splendid plans. That the moment that one definitely commits oneself then providence moves too. All sorts of things to help one that would never otherwise have occurred manifest themselves. A whole stream of events issue from the decision, raising in one's favor all manner of unforeseen incidents and meetings and material assistances that no man could have dreamed would have come his way."
- W.H. Murray

Let's Talk About Results

What are the results you've been getting in your trading and in your life? If they are less than what you want, if they, in fact, suck (to use a non-technical term), then changes are in order—from the inside out, changes that involve new strategies for thinking, which in turn create room for forming effective habits and controlling errant emotions. Results, any results, follow a model and that model is sequential. In fact, let's call it The Results Model. The Results Model begins with an event. An event is anything that gets your attention. For instance, you wake up and realize the alarm didn't go off. You had set it to alert you to an early Economic Calendar report, but now you missed the play. That's an event. You turn on your computer and somehow your connection isn't working, so you can't get your data. That's an event. Your significant other reminds you of a chore you promised to do that you've forgotten about and the timing has come back to bite you. That's an event. Your number one son comes home from school sporting a tattoo—on his face. That's an event. Events are, for the most part, 'message neutral'; they have no meaning aside from what we ascribe to them.

Every event has three components:

1) What is it?

2) What does it mean to me?

3) What am I going to do about it?

It's as though a camera has snapped a picture of the event, and multiple people seeing that same picture which each have their own interpretation of the event, because we all come from different experiences.

The next point in the model involves our MAPS (a phrase coined from Peter Senge's book *The Fifth Discipline*). MAPs are mental models or paradigms of the environment. MAPS are not an acronym and only refer to all that we have learned from 0 years up to and including the present moment. These MAPS are largely out of our awareness because they draw from programmed lessons stemming from our earliest days. They are similar to the "operating system" of a computer; that is to say, the underlying program the software is driven by. These lessons or "programs" are derived from family members, teachers, coaches, counselors, TV, radio, friends, and enemies—anyone that has ever been significant to us in any way. All of our experiences go into the mix. These programs create the lenses or "filters" through which we see the world. They work automatically and immediately. And, they are very much like maps we would use to direct our travel. The map is only as good as the information. The map is bound by the limits of the book or page. The map is "not" the terrain; it is only a representation.

Our MAPS, or "filters" if you will, are only as accurate as the lessons that we learned. Consequently, if one grew up being told that rich people are greedy, money-grubbing jerks who take advantage of others, the picture, however inaccurate, becomes the "unconscious mythology" that drives conscious thoughts about money and people who have money. Furthermore, if you grew up in a household with an alcoholic father and a clinically depressed mother, your view of the world is filtered by or bound by those childhood experiences . And, finally, these mental models, filters or thought patterns become ingrained as though they were the "truth" about life, rather than a "representation" of what we've been taught about life, so that our mythology or our underlying thinking is acted upon as though it were reality.

Next, we draw conclusions, form interpretations, and make meaning of the event based upon those MAPS or mental models after the event is filtered through them. Depending on how deep and strong the mythology is, it will determine how strongly we react or respond when they have been activated. The truth may be miles from what we think, but our reaction can be immediate, unwavering, and unmistakable to us. Consider the phrase, "You look like your father." Now, if your father was a loving, respectful, giving, nurturing and strong man, those positive images would be your internal picture as soon as the phrase was uttered—and your response, I suggest, would be in keeping with the positive picture that is just below the surface (warm and very positive). If on the other hand, your father was mean, cruel, shiftless, lazy and abusive, and someone mentions tells you how closely you resemble him, your response—based upon your internal model of what "father" means to you—might be very different. I am suggesting that the conclusions we draw, and the meaning we give to events, are based upon those internal MAPS. These can and often do create immediate, automatic and autocratic responses. In fact, the more deeply seated the mythology or MAPS, and the more frequently they are activated, the more intractable the behavioral "patterns" we act out.

What we *think* determines our emotions. When we react or respond, there are essentially three emotional domains we face:

1) Positive emotions –we feel glad, happy, giving, receptive, included, and or loving.

2) Neutral emotions –we really don't have any emotional investment and don't care. Feeling nonchalant, uninvolved, and or disinterested.

3) Other than positive or neutral emotions –anger, sadness, jealousy, envy, guilt, fear and greed.

Obviously, the first two domains garner a very different behavioral response than the third. If I were angry, jealous, envious or sad, my behavioral response is likely not going to be as warm and fuzzy as if I were glad, happy, receptive or simply disinterested.

Results are the consequences and outcomes when the event is filtered through the layers of MAPS. When interpretations and assumptions are made, conclusions are drawn, emotions are activated based on mythology and meaning, and a behavior is generated. Let's see how this might play out. It's early morning and you are walking down the hallway at work. You come upon your buddy, with whom you have a relationship. You are good friends. Just as you say hello with a smile and are about to stop and possibly chat, he walks right by and completely ignores you. Now, you may not be in a great mood to begin with. What do you think a normal thought might be? "That *&^%)$% didn't even speak. He really insulted me." What feelings do you think would underlie that kind of thinking? Most people might say anger, rejection and hurt, right? And, of course, this response came immediately and decisively, right from the book of "Hey, he can't treat me that way. What's his problem?" But what if I told you that the person walking by just found out that a close family member was in a bad accident and was hospitalized. Would that have any bearing on your interpretations, assumptions, and conclusions? Of course it would. If you're like most normal people, you would feel an immediate compassion, and you would understand that his reaction to your morning greeting wasn't personal, nor with this new interpretation would you feel hurt or angry. Now, did the event change? No, it didn't. The only thing that changed was the *meaning* of the event. If a video camera had shot the event all we would have seen would have been two people passing in the hallway. One spoke and the other didn't. So, in this vignette, we can see that what is often deemed reality or the facts are often neither.

So how does this apply to trading? Well, we can easily get caught up in an event. Does this sound familiar? The price pattern you see might look like it "must" be a symmetrical triangle or a double top and you enter into the trade "knowing" that it "must" be about to move in "this" direction. Then the tick goes against you and you feel a sense of panic and dread. You haven't put a stop loss in and the price action makes a sudden and dramatic move. You begin to get high on "hopium," the drug traders grab when the price action has moved significantly in the opposite direction from their target, and they begin to hope that it comes back—and worse, they may double down in the position attempting to get back to break-even. Later, and maybe *much* later, they go back to look at the trade set-up again and, lo and behold, it looks nothing like the set-up they got into. Or, something else has appeared that they never saw the first time around. In any event, in the "excitement" to make the trade, the "reality" was distorted by the greed of making more money or the fear of losing again, to the point that an illusion or delusion took place. In other words, the results reflected the state of mind they were in and this, for so many, becomes a pattern played out over and over again.

As you can see, the results we experience can be traced directly to how and what we think. If you are getting results that fly in the face of what you want, then you must change your thinking to break the pattern in which you've found yourself. As the cliché goes, the definition of insanity is continuing to do the same thing but expecting a different result. Change your thinking to change your results, because if you always do what you've always done, you'll always get what you've always gotten.

Shark Infested Waters: Why it's Crucial to Have Self-Discipline

"If you bring forth what is within you, what you bring forth will save you. If you do not bring forth what is within you, what you do not bring forth will destroy you." - Gospel of Thomas

Understanding Zero-Sum

The market exists because of conflict. For every transaction, there must be a buyer and a seller; hence, it is necessarily adversarial, and in each individual transaction there can only be one winner; the other must lose. It is impossible for both sides to be right and the order flow goes in only 2 directions, up or down. Even in a sideways market, when you look closely, you'll notice that the tick or pip goes up, then down, which only means that there are equal numbers of buyers and sellers at each order. So, the importance of knowing the order flow cannot be overstated.

"At some point both winner and loser must exit the market. – they must at some point close the trade to turn a debit/credit into a case settlement. Approximately 85 – 90% of price action is the loser liquidating. Only the loser "must" execute. The winner can wait because he is not under threat. When the loser and winner execute and leave the market; the market is vulnerable to a reversal – only winners are left. The market is a neutral organic reflection of buyer/seller conflict that will never end as long as the market exists. All price action is determined by an imbalance of orders overtime. How and when those orders are placed (and filled) creates what you see as price action." – Janson Alan Jankovsky, *Psychology of Trading*

Winning at Zero Sum

Your order must be ahead of the next wave of order-flow in the direction that will be a reflection of the price action. One hundred percent of your market study must be designed to find where the eventual loser will be placing his orders – nothing else matters in your study. Where is the loser now and to where will he be moving?

Psychology of Price Action

Price action is about pain or pleasure. Price action begins in the mind of every trader just as she decides to make a play. She has enough conviction in making that trade to put herself at risk. She believes (if he is trading) and hopes (if he is gambling) that he will make a profit; otherwise, he would not make the trade. The question is "What creates that belief, and what happens when, due to the failure of his decision, he must change that belief?" If you are wrong and price moves against you, there is pain. When the pain is strong enough, you will get out. Pain takes place as soon as there is realization that the conflict between the desire to make money and the fact that the trade is in the wrong place has been made. Pain is directly proportional to the momentum of price action and the degree of real estate or space from the entry. As it moves away from your losing entry, the pain grows until you liquidate and leave the market. If the winner has done the same, there are less people in the market, but only one thing is certain: only the winner can afford to wait to liquidate as time goes on. Even if prices stop moving against the loser, his pain grows, because he thinks to himself, "The trade is not working. I can't wait anymore." The conflict of price action is also driven by pressure, buying and selling.

The market is only a neutral organic representation of the price action; the pain is not created by, nor is it in, the market. It is only in the head of the trader. Therefore you *are* the market. There are those who would like to think that the market is "against them," and that it is somehow a fight, but the fight is really with yourself.

The order flow we've been describing is created by each trader, the buyers and sellers, and the pressures of each. How the order flow comes in natural imbalance, and this imbalance, becomes the price action. Knowing where the loser is in the order flow is all that we need to concern ourselves with when we trade: "Where is the loser and when will he quit?"

What does this mean? Well, we start the process of understanding what our particular starting point is and what prevents us from seeing where the loser is because we *are* the loser at this point. In many ways, our thinking is the same as every other loser out there. Knowing how we think gives us clues to how they think. We then learn to separate ourselves from the crowd.

Seeing Reality Vs. the Distortion of Desire for Profit

"The goal of inner work is to help clients unblock their bottlenecks and learn how to live in partnership with the unconscious rather than at its mercy." -Fritz Kunkle

The Importance of Rules to Avoid Self-Sabotage

Humans live by the stories they have constructed from early in life, much like actors following a script to a play. That play is your life, and the scripts to that play are your stories. These stories or scripts can also be termed *rules* that form the foundation of our behavior. In fact, as humans grow, they develop a set of typical responses to reoccurring events. These responses or patterns of behavior can be termed *a list of rules* that we live by. For example, when someone speaks to me, it is customary, and my pattern, that I will speak back. If I incur a debt, I will pay it. If I am driving in the streets, there is a set of rules that I follow for both safety and the orderly movement of traffic. These lists of "rules", social mores or cultural myths we have incorporated are reflected in every decision and aspect of our lives. They are often unconscious. They involve lessons we have learned in life and, therefore, the cultural lenses we have unwittingly created through which we see and judge the world.

Many of these 'rules' revolve around money, privilege, power, worthiness, esteem, competency, winning and the need to do or have it now. For the most part, these stories or rules of living never see the light of day in our consciousness. In other words, if our choices go unchallenged, then the awareness of why we chose that thought and/or behavior remains out of conscious touch. However, once the rule is identified, it can be challenged and modified as needed. Also, as we challenge each rule, we uncover other assumptions based upon that rule being truth rather than myth. The interesting thing about mythology is that we believe it to be real. To us, it is not mythology; it is truth. Consider this: trader Dan believes in "taking advantage of every opportunity in life." This belief becomes truth in his mind and generally may not be a problem for him. However, in the markets there is a distinct disadvantage to overtrading. In fact, this simple yet powerful "myth" can cause your downfall in trading even though it can serve you in life.

Other "Fool's Rules" or trading myths might be:

- Get back to even by doubling down on losers

- On a price action pattern, jump in early to make the most profit

- Stops only take me out too early; it will always come back

- Big position size makes big money

- I can trade as many times a day as I want; the more I trade, the more opportunities

- I have to make money

Because the market is a unique cultural phenomenon, it does not resonate with most accepted cultural myths, and usually our life-rules only lead to accurate identification of order flow by accident. So, for the most part, the filter or mental model you have will frequently conclude something inaccurate unless you re-program the MAP that it came from. That's why intelligent and educated people can succeed at any other business and fail at trading because the usually effective life-model that works in the real world is not the same paradigm that creates price action. So, to re-program, we must uncover the MAPS, mental models, and paradigms that we use. We must identify where they show up in daily trading;

consider the above example of overtrading that stems from a potentially unconscious belief around taking advantage of every opportunity. If we examine it even closer, we might uncover a fear associated with missing out on a perceived potential profit and, below that, may reside the fear of appearing not smart enough or good enough. The way that it might show up is this trading journal excerpt: "...*I'm dealing with the thought that ' I've got to get in on this trade' or 'I've got to make up for the last loss' ... No, I do not "have" to force a trade in order to make up for the last loss". I will wait for the next high probability, compelling set-up to trade and if it doesn't come along today then that's OK – I'm a lover of reality."*

One of the ways we fall prey to self-sabotage is trading from rules that don't work, and these rules may be all or partly unconscious. Most have experienced self-sabotage, also known as 'shooting yourself in the foot'. It is behavior in direct contradiction to what you know to be in your best interest.

Does the following sound familiar? *Jack has a high profile leadership position. His job demands that he create a year-end report. Jack is well aware of the large amount of effort and time it takes to competently deliver this report, and every year Jack will wait till the last minute, incurring unnecessary stress and mental anguish, not to mention lost sleep, to get it in on time. However, due to the sensitive nature of this report, on more than one occasion Jack has missed important data and, except for some after-the-fact machinations, jeopardized the accuracy and reliability of the effort. As a consequence of this behavior, Jack has failed to get a plum promotion to the executive floor, even though he clearly has performed well in many areas and has the skills to do the executive job.*

Consider this example: *Tracy knows the value of identifying the trend, locating significant support and resistance, and waiting for retracements in order to discover high probability entries. In fact, her Trading Rules specifically state that before entering she will pause, check all time frames, recheck support/resistance levels, and wait for a retracement on a trending market. However, with the rise of a high momentum green candle on the 5-minute chart, the excitement gets the best of her and she impulsively enters, only to immediately watch it retrace and stop her out for a loss. Upon looking back at the trade, she then realizes that there was a doji candle at a significant resistance level on the 15-minute chart signaling a high-probability reversal. If she had followed her Trading Rules, she would have been following the order flow, identifying where the loser is likely to trade and she would have taken the other side to be in sync with the order flow.*

The meaning here is that self-sabotaging behavior looms on the horizon at every turn, and unless measures are taken to increase your awareness of your own internal mythology, you will most likely execute in the wrong spot relative to actual order flow, turning what initially promises to be a winner into a loser. You can't change what you can't face, and you can't face what you don't know. Hence, we need a Thought Journal to discover thought patterns and raise awareness of internal mythology to engage in a "dance with the market." In this way, we are able to follow the lead of the order flow. It takes diligence, consistency, and time to first become aware and, second, to change ineffective patterns. A Thought Journal helps through questions like these:

- What is my analysis of this trade?

- Why do I want to enter at this point in the order flow?

- What is my target and why did I choose it?

- Why do I trust my analysis?

- Who told me it would work and why do I believe it?

- Who is showing up to trade today?

- What is my emotional temperature?

- What are my thoughts?

And as you delve deeper into the morass of your strongly held beliefs, some of these questions are very important as well:

- What does money represent to me?

- From where do my beliefs about money come?

- If I experience a substantial draw down what, if anything, does it say about me?

- Who am I in this trade?

A Thought Journal can be hand-written or typed, on a notepad or input into a log along with daily inputs of trade results. In the Appendix, there is an example of a Trade Journal and what it might look like.

Beware of *comparisons of the answers*, that is, comparisons with another trader or with yourself in another trade. Comparing is fraught with judgment that can actually be driven by an unconscious bias pushing unwanted behavior. You are unique and have your own challenges, strengths, improvables, learning process and perspective. This is a part of mythology. Additionally, every trade has its own variables and trade components. How you were and what was going on in a previous trade may not be useful as a comparison to how and what you did in your last trade. What is useful is to find the patterns of your thinking and increase your awareness of inner drives. Furthermore, comparison, especially with others, holds no critical or useful information to your thinking. It distracts from the important issue at hand, which essentially is: "What are my mental models, MAPS and paradigms about trading or the trade?" It simply doesn't matter how well or how dismally someone else is doing. It doesn't matter how they learn, or what they are challenged by. It doesn't matter what they think of your issues or how you trade. What matters is you. What is your one-of-a-kind makeup? This doesn't mean you can't learn from someone else. It doesn't mean you can't find similarities between your way of learning and perceiving and someone else's. It doesn't mean you can't be mentored or guided, or that someone can't be your role model. What it does mean is simply that comparing your progress with someone else's does not serve you.

Introspection can be arduous and scary. That is why so many people avoid self-examination, but it is where the treasure trove of personal information lies. There is value in becoming aware of unwanted proclivities and subsequently identifying strategies to address the improvables. In other words, it is paramount to discover where the fault lines lie in your behavioral landscape so you can be prepared to ward off an impending mental/emotional quake. These disturbances in your mental topography are forces that disrupt and distort reality and lead to F.E.A.R: False Events Appearing Real.

Finding Your Achilles Heel

"All disorders serve as messengers for us to learn from." - Australian Aboriginal
Teaching

Awareness and Reprogramming

In order to seize the results and outcomes we desire, we must have clarity of
thought, clarity of vision and consistency of effective behavior. And, of course,
your prior programming has enormous importance to the rubric of daily activity
you wade through to achieve those results. Let us turn to how addressing the
factors and forces that rob you of clear thinking, clear sight and right behavior.
Before we can think, see and do with effectiveness, we must be aware of our
improveables, or those underlying self-sabotaging rules. This may seem
obvious, and to many it is, but there are large numbers of people wandering
aimlessly through life without a clue. As they say, you don't know what you
don't know. That pertains directly to knowing and not knowing about yourself.
One of the ways to become better acquainted with yourself, especially some of
those deeply held myths and unconscious beliefs that drive your thinking,
perception and behavior, is to write about your experiences using a thought
journal. Through the thought journal, you gain insight into "why" you have not
developed a coherent trading plan or haven't followed the plan that you've
created. The thought journal reveals why you violated your rules or why you
haven't established any. You'll have a better understanding of "why" you
haven't established a money management strategy or aren't following it when
oversized positions are entered leading to the mother-of-all-drawdowns. Once
you learn the *why*, you will be in a better position to change your behavior. That
doesn't mean that you can't change faulty behavior unless it is completely
analyzed and laid out; yes, there are those who only need an example of effective
behavior, and they are off and running. If you are that person, then my

suggestion is to run, don't walk, to your nearest successful mentor for help .
However, many if not most, traders are plagued with those errant emotions
spoken of earlier; that is, the abject fear and rampant greed that hogties those that
know what to do but can't do it due to their emotions.

Once you have identified and recognized an errant or ineffective paradigm,
mental model or MAP, it's time to evaluate the extent to which it disrupts your
perception of reality. Next, you must restructure or modify the paradigm or
mythology in order to "see" clearly. Gains or losses on any one trade must be
evaluated from a new point of view. Otherwise, you cannot know with certainty
that you properly executed the trade based upon what the chart is providing. If
you don't know what went wrong, it can't be modified and therefore change
cannot happen; you can't duplicate positive action or prevent negative action.
You want to accumulate profit and that is about learning to do more right things
than wrong things, as well as possessing the knowledge to know the difference.
It's important to redefine how we measure gain versus loss, or, more specifically,
results. It's not about making money; it's about remaining consistent with what
matters most in the price action, mainly consistently doing what keeps you on the
right side of the order flow. If money is made by accident, it's nearly like taking
a loss, because you didn't learn from the trade and therefore you can't duplicate
the behavior.

If evaluation of the trade is determined solely by money made or lost, the value
has been placed on a transient result and not a principle. In and of itself, money
is only a medium. It is not grounded in a consistent truth or foundation. It is
dependent upon consensus for its value. Conversely, processes based on
principle, that is, a guiding fundamental truth, promote a deep common

denominator forging a pathway for creating consistent results. These are the kind of results that stem from accurately identifying the reality of the chart or price action in order to be on the right side of the order flow. For instance, the principle of self-disciplined learning and awareness of how closely you accurately perceive the reality of the trade (a market principle) as opposed to the inconsistent distortion based upon seeing what you want to see (an ineffective behavior based upon internal mythology).

Where do breakdowns in perception come from and where are losses generated? They come from interpretations based upon faulty conclusions or construing meanings not aligned with reality. If, for example, you:

1) "See" a symmetrical triangle that appears to have formed over three months...

2) "Believe" it is going to break to the upside...

3) Get excited and impulsively buy a long option with only 1 month of time because it's *going* to break soon...

4) Don't need to pay the extra premium for time...

...then you have just allowed your emotions (excitement and greed) to misguide your perception. You enter the trade with behavior based upon distorted emotions. You have a rule about always buying 2 or 3 months and, if the price pattern considered takes several months to form, then your rule says you should buy more time, but you ignore the trading rule with a rationalization. Part of what you *tell* yourself is that it *should* break-up and *should* do it soon because it is so *perfect*. You begin to *should* on yourself. Language like should, shouldn't, must, can't, and gonna all have one thing in common: they are not based in fact but are based on assumption, MSU's, which create F.E.A.R.--False Events

Appearing Real. So, based upon what you see, you enter the trade and, as soon as you do, the price action goes the other way; it drops precipitously. And, of course, you panic and grab the hopium, hoping it will come back. And it does, 6 weeks later, long after the option has expired and you have taken a good loss. Now the only *should* applicable here is that you should have lost. Yes, you should have lost. Because, based upon the conditions and circumstances present, you bought just the right amount of time, responded to just the right amount of assumptions, and engaged just the right execution in order to crash and burn. The universe is based on cause and effect. You created the cause through flawed logic based upon inaccurate data, and disregarded important facts. It's like the law of gravity. If we drop something it will fall until operated upon by an intervening variable, like the floor. How do we know that? Because it does. How do we know we should have lost? Because we did. We get the results we should get based upon the circumstances and conditions present. The definition of insanity is expecting a different result when we keep doing the same thing, continuing to trade using the strategy of loss, i.e., "put my head down and barrel forward disregarding my rules and going on what I *think*—in other words, "gambling."

And what if the price action goes in our direction? How can you know this was not an accident? You know this by interpretations based upon the chart and by following your rules. And, when there is no emotional conflict, the goal is to remain in the process of self-awareness during the entire trade. The successful result is a function of self-awareness, not money gained. If you realize you are duplicating losing behavior, exit, even if the trade has a profit. By exiting the market when you are duplicating losing behavior, you eliminate the potential for accidental profits, which give the *illusion* of true skill. With a focus on the commitment to effective protocols, you foster skill building and make your *self* available for new learning opportunities. You want to enhance capacity for skill building by not supporting unskilled market machinations—even when profitable. You want to only support behavior that is goal or skill oriented so that this skill is strengthened and honed.

Many who venture into the world of financial markets to be a trader are successful in other places in their lives. But the habits and traits that caused you to be successful in, say, the corporate world have the opposite effect on trading. Rather than being support mechanisms, many are downright liabilities. For instance, working hard in a trade will only lead to stress and constriction. Working hard is antithetical to being relaxed, calm and centered. Another is being good at multi-tasking; multi-tasking, even if you can track your trades well, leads to over-exposure in the market and quickly violates money management rules. Being fast and finishing quickly, a great snatcher of money in the market. You can't rush the market. It moves, travels and dances to it's own rhythm and pace. Additionally, you won't and can't force a trade through will or sheer power of personality. The market cares nothing about how much money you have or not—either it is in the set-up or it is not.

Record Keeping

Market action must never influence your position or willingness to act. The converse is true as well. If you are following your rules, you first determine your position based upon the price action. However, after you have initiated a plan, the market action must not unduly influence your position or willingness to act. You must exit the market when you sense you are distorting market information through fear, greed, hope, pain, or any other emotion including euphoria from past wins. Your point of view must always be to protect yourself first, no matter what is going on in the market. Because you are looking for the point in the market where the order flow will change, you must learn how to tell when you are most likely unable to see that, and either not trade or liquidate your position. By removing yourself from the market, you create more information about yourself, your thinking, the market structure and your willingness or unwillingness to act.

Using self-examination along with market observation, you develop a focal clarity supported by a calmer demeanor, and a more relaxed state that mitigates the stress of having money at risk. Risk and the prospect of loss prompt anxiety; however, this emotion can be contained through the stress management techniques outlined later in the book. In this way, you will be able to resonate with reality and see the market price action without the distortion of your own wishes. What to do next becomes self-evident at that point. Once you know why you do what you do and the way you do it, trading becomes effortless, a series of habitual behaviors that are rules- based. By maintaining the issue of observation, not evaluation, your true trading strengths or weaknesses become known to you. My good friend is a communications consultant who specializes in training people how to effectively have "difficult conversations." He instructs them to "say what you see" in order to neutralize the emotional judgment that comes from making assumptions about another's intent. The markets are best approached in that same way. They don't care about you in the least, but many traders want to attribute intent to the price action or they want to think, hope, assume, and/or feel that they know where the market is going. Instead of doing that, "say what you see" in the price action and follow its lead. The benefit you receive is learning to stay out of the market when win probabilities are low, and trading when probabilities are high. You will cut losses fast and you will have a high percentage of trades that work quickly. You will have a few that go your way long and hard.

How to get there? Write out your rules and post them prominently so they can easily be seen as you trade. Read them every day before trading. Create empowering self-talk by writing down affirmative statements regarding entries/exits and when to be in and when to be out of the market. Write statements about your ability to "see" the price action for what it is. Also, be sure to journal every day. By putting your trades and thoughts down, you learn more about what works and thereby prime yourself for success and support consistency in performance. Profits accumulate just as surely as losing trades when the process protocol is followed with religious fervor. No trader has 100% winners as far as money growth is concerned. Money growth is the result of trading as a 100% winner; where the definition of winner is "I follow my rules." In that way, you are disciplined to protect yourself first.

By seeing trading not as 'money made or lost' but discipline performed or not, your potential to access your true trading strengths becomes higher. As you increase your knowledge of those strengths and trade from them, your money results will reflect that; beginning with, "losing a lot less."

Examples of positive self-talk:

- I clearly see the market price action and market information
- I follow my rules with a passion and hold on like grasping a life line

- I accept that losses are part of the game. If I have lost but kept my rules, I feel positive and productive because I know that the path to success is through following my rules

- I value myself enough to cut a loss. I know I have done the right thing for me

- I journal every day and after every trade. I value myself enough to get the data I need to win

Keeping good records provides crucial data for long-term growth and success. Keeping your trade records is crucial for understanding the order-flow, crucial for understanding price action and crucial for increasing self-awareness; for instance, where we are weak and strong. Document your trading and review the data for clues of whether or not you're on track. This process forms a "feedback loop."

The Feedback Loop – What Goes Around Comes Around

The feedback loop is a checklist or roadmap to compare your desired state of awareness against your actual state of awareness. In order to make your trading home in the desired "trading state," you'll want to remain fully present and in the "now" of the trade. The goal is to stay focused and in an optimum trading position, emotionally and mentally on the path that leads to consistent profitability by constant anticipation of what may take us off course and vigilant about what will keep us on course.

Setting a course is much different from staying on course. They both require a different set of skills. Because we are involved in an arena under a constant state of inequality, which changes moment-to-moment, the need for vigilance is critical to staying on course. The Feedback Loop or trade cycle is the daily moment-to-moment state of mind that leads to the greatest success your trade approach can deliver. The goal is to make your trading protocol a lifestyle. You and your trading are the same thing because whatever traits you exhibit before and after the trade are those traits that will express during the trade. The point is to embellish those habits that are supportive and diminish those that aren't. Report every trade detail, including the nuances. You are pursuing consistency and the creation of supportive habits, not thinking. Consistent, positive behavior comes from the creation of and the support of positive habits, positive habits are not "thought" into existence. Thought supports their creation, but thought alone will never instill a habit. For example, we may know that we have a tendency to be in fear about our trading. We may know that it pressures us to make impulsive moves, but until we document how that is happening, we lack the data to modify our behavior with confidence.

Thought Journal/Trade Journal

A Thought Journal is designed to reveal destructive and constructive thought patterns. A Trade Journal is designed to reveal our self-destructive behaviors and our positive behaviors. Human beings are impulsively driven by greed and the desire to dominate. They will take the easiest way to get and keep what they want. This often has negative and unintended consequences that are frequently destructive. And humans are not naturally prone to accountability or self-discipline, which is why we need laws, rules, boundaries, and limits in society. Trading requires self-imposed limits and these limits must be created through personal accountability. We must know what we need in order to create effective self-limits or self-control. Documenting actual behavior provides the data to compare to our thinking and to identify strength and weakness—thinking precedes behavior and behavior reflects thinking. When you accurately record the thinking that was present during a trade, it exposes your actual state of mind, not the desired state or the one that we tell ourselves we have already. This confronts illusion about our true skill. Some of the things to look for are:

- Was my stop/limit hit or did I take myself out?

- How much time was I in the trade?

Then compare your recorded thoughts to your trade plan:

- Where are the inconsistencies?

- Where are the congruencies?

- Is anything different than what I planned or expected?

It's very important to identify the weaknesses and the strengths of your execution. After that, new habits and supportive behaviors can be created.

It is critically important to identify the faulty patterns of thinking causing the errant behavior. After identifying the bad behavior, isolate it by creating rules to follow. When the rule has been created, use mental techniques like EFT and NLP (to be explained later) to help support effective ways to modify the bad behavior one trade at a time. Thought and emotions are difficult to control. The difficulty stems from the deep seated and unconscious nature of the programmed patterns that cause the unwanted behavior to begin with. The goal is to get into a mental place to see how the behavior reflected foggy thinking and how thoughts and emotions work together to create results—this knowledge helps create a rule designed to cut losses and position you to re-observe the order flow without the emotional interference.

Personality is an amalgam; that is, we have many parts to us that don't always get along. Our personality is formed through the learned achievements and learned limitations that are presented through our MAPs and personal mythology. The "parts," so to speak, are sub-personalities formed through patterning and strategies as a response to certain environmental conditions. For instance, we may act differently with our fathers than with our mothers, especially if we didn't grow up with one or the other. It is also likely that we have a different persona at the office than at home. And, we may act differently when stressed and under pressure than when we are relaxed and unthreatened.

Different sides reflect different program patterns. We are not always the same and how we are is based upon what part of us shows up. Also, the environment, biorhythms, discomfort vs. comfort, recent events that may have shaken our confidence, or caused other than positive or neutral emotions, all have an impact upon who shows up. So, sometimes we are confident and relaxed; sometimes we are agitated and anxious; sometimes we are depressed and fatalistic. Deep-seated MAPs or mental models create these emotions. They result in "who is coming to the trade today" and greatly affect how events are perceived. In other words, are you perceiving the reality of the chart? The goal is to get on the right side of the order flow. The order flow is a natural and free flowing phenomena and it is an open-ended system that resonates with itself. The ideal as a trader is to approach the market system in an open and available state, and in balance with oneself and resonating with the organic aspects of the market system. We want to be affirming and focused on supporting our effectiveness, in part by accepting whatever the reality is externally. It's about becoming one with the organic market forces. This means remaining in a constant state of observation, whether getting in or staying out *or* staying in or getting out.

Full participation in the market means perpetual observation, whether in a trade or not. There is no attachment to any price action because you are only watching it. There are no emotions because nothing is different from moment to moment. Embracing the unceasing undulations of the market as never ending creates a mindset and framework that supports your ability to be in harmony with it. You are able to move in and out of the market because you become one with it, part and parcel to its reality.

When you do something that you enjoy, like riding a bike, you can choose to ride or not ride, and you can ride as long as you want, riding easy or energetically. The laws of centrifugal force remain the same. A long as you pedal, you will continue to ride, and if you stop, the laws still continue. By embracing the market as perpetual motion of an organic system with never-ending unfolding events, in harmony with itself, you are better positioned to approach it with the internal harmony of your highest and best self. The question is "How close to my highest and best self am I at this moment?" The market is constant (like centrifugal force). You don't need to be concerned with the market. You just need to be fully present, in that moment, and available for it. There is no right, wrong, good, bad, should, must, can't, hope, fear, pain, or other hyperbolic emotional moniker that can rightfully be attributed to the market system. "Things are as they are and I am the way I am. I am always participating. It is what it is and I am what I am."

Your Thought Journal and Trade Journal work together to confront weaknesses and consolidate strengths. You create new rules to modify your behavior until you sense you are in the feedback loop of the trade. As you consistently support your effectiveness by building your strengths and consistently minimizing your weaknesses, you become more and more aligned with what the market is—a natural system. Waiting and watching is a form of participation in the market. Becoming symbiotic with this natural system is to watch the price action breath and move. With experience, and by increasing your capacity for internal alignment between your parts through journal work, you and the market can become aligned. When this happens, you see the order flow as it is and not as you "wish" it would be. Then you may choose to get in. If you sense you are not aligned, you get out. But whether you are aligned or not, you are always getting in or getting out, depending on the needs you have at that moment.

The Feedback Loop provides a roadmap and blueprint of where you want to go and what you want to build in your trading so you can accurately see and participate in the order flow without being overly influenced by emotional interference. The objective of emotional interference is not to eliminate it. Emotions are an inextricable part of who we are as human beings. The point is to learn how to understand more about them so they can be contained and controlled to a degree, ultimately seen as an ally to boost the drive to stay on course so behavior and performance are not adversely affected. As you modify both cause and effect, you know where that modification is leading. By knowing your strengths and weaknesses as a trader, knowing the state you want to achieve, and knowing you are on the path to getting there, you close the gap between you and the market. Your natural ability to perform, and the market's natural ability to perform ,are better aligned, and the correct action to take next is self-evident. Get in, stay in or get out, stay out.

The Zen of Trading

"Success usually comes to those who are too busy to be looking for it" -
Henry David Thoreau (1817-1862)

How you show up to trade is a process of consistency and equates to a lifestyle
issue. Due to the nature of the markets, they are not a place to visit to make
money; they are where you express yourself. Trading is an art form; you express
yourself through every pattern of behavior that either supports or negates the
effectiveness of the artful dance. The point here is to emphasize that self-
discipline is a function of diligence and vigilance in the process. Without them
you would do better to find an occupation that doesn't require as much self-
discipline and would be a lot less stress strain and money out of your jeans.

Identifying Patterns When Things Go Right, Not Just Poorly

The feedback loop is supportive for "what works" not just "what doesn't work"
as a way to identify issues and patterns in our behavior. When trading is going
well, what are your behaviors? It's important to identify a successful pattern of
behaviors and thoughts, then to follow that pattern as a "model," replicating each
thought and behavior. So, what we're talking about is identifying the times when
trading was going well and using your self as the subject. And, of course, it's not
about emulating a trading guru. It's about examining patterns for both obstacles
and supports. Finding solutions means enacting them consistently, not just
knowing what to do but also doing it; in other words, developing powerful
habits.

Some of these strong and powerful habits are:

- Learning to sustain purpose

- Remaining on task

- Developing a strong sensory rich vision

- Being intentional around your plan

- Being careful of living to trade, rather than trading to live

Addictions are problematic. Addictive behavior causes impulsivity and compulsivity. You become prone to force trades. Rather, you want to foster a compelling reason for each trade based upon the reality of the charts. The thought journal can be used to flush out addictive patterns.

Manage Emotional Distress by Managing Current Life Challenges

- It isn't necessary to change your personality to make major life changes. The challenge is to make your personality work for you, rather than against you. Playing to win, rather than playing not to lose, is part of the foundational answer. Focus on specific patterns you want to alter. Use the rifle approach, not the shotgun, by targeting the specifics—for instance:

- Impulsivity
- Fear of entering positions
- Inconsistency in risk management

Traders change when they leverage their achievement orientation as a solution and stop beating themselves up and endlessly analyzing their flaws. Don't define yourself as the problem and thereby use your own achievement orientation to turn on yourself; rather, use asset-based thinking to maximize your best and focus on the next.

There are Pivot Points in your patterns (up and down, effective and ineffective) just like pivot points in a chart. There are pivot points and changes that come as a result of stimuli (either internal or external) that initiate a pivot point in your patterns. Music, as with other stimuli, can be used to activate a personal pivot point, just as market forces can cause a pivot point in the charts. Identifying music that is uplifting and motivational, resonates with you and has a point in it that creates a "pattern interrupt" can create a mood shift, just as doing something different can be anchored to create a mood shift. For example, identifying something you know will elicit a pleasant experience, remembering the experience, anchoring it, and then using the anchor to reinitiate the state that carries with it all the encoded sensory input activated during the anchored event. The anchored event could be a memory of achievement, a slammin' vacation or a seminal event in your life, like having a baby or getting married.

The anchor can be used to interrupt an ineffective pattern causing emotional distress or unsupportive behavior, such as impulsive entries and exits or breaking your established rules. Patterns can also be interrupted by other events, choreographed or otherwise; for instance, a crying baby will stop crying if a loud noise or other interesting stimuli comes into her purview, just as a piece of music that is uplifting and energizing can create a pattern interrupt, since it serves to shift the level of consciousness and positively expand the focus to take in more of the reality of the charts. Musically speaking, this can be seen as the abrupt shift in a pivot chord that changes the mood and breaks the pattern, as laughter will often completely diffuse an angry outburst. It's impossible to be angry and laugh at the same time; they are contravening emotions. Unsupportive patterns can also be termed ineffective routines.

Patterns and routines as noted above could habituate when an environmental event consistently presents itself, such as the abusive alcoholic father who strikes fear into the heart of the child. The thought-emotion-behavior dynamic associated with these recurring events would habituate and become patterns and routines. The thoughts and emotions lodge principally in the right brain, where darker, pain-filled, negative events are deposited. Also, the right hemisphere is intuitive, global, circular in logic, and largely unconscious. The left hemisphere is linear in logic, vertical thinking, tangible, and largely conscious—the lighter side of the two hemispheres. Patterns and routines, especially those associated with MAPs and paradigms learned in negative life events, not only tend to habituate and become somewhat "hard-wired" in the brain, but are also associated with emotional states driven by unconscious thoughts. This is why we might hit our heads after a particularly "bone-headed" trade where we thought we saw something that wasn't there, or didn't see something that was there and otherwise did not resonate with the reality of the price action data. Right-brain mediated interventions are pattern interrupts and highly supportive techniques and exercises that can help to bring awareness to the behavior or help shift our thinking, expand consciousness, re-establish relaxation, focus positive energy and promote the oneness with the market we need. The following are examples of right-brain mediated interventions:

- Role-playing
- Meditation
- Self-hypnosis
- Trance

- Dance

- Thought journaling

- Stretching

- Music

- Dream analysis

- Storytelling

Let's look at it another way. Internal states are created by major events in our lives, positive and negative, pleasurable and painful. When something highly pleasurable or painful happens, neurochemicals are released in the brain that encode (memory stamp) the information in a state-bound way. This is termed State Bound Learning Memory and Behavior. Whenever the memory of the events (the abuse from the alcoholic father) is triggered by similar stimuli in the environment, then the state—which includes all the sensory data experienced in the original event—is activated in a rush of feelings and thoughts. So, the errant pattern is a specific state or mood. Interrupt the pattern and you interrupt the state and thereby create the opportunity to shift to another supportive and productive state. This causes a shift in the thought-emotion-behavior dynamic. This shift can be positively designed and "anchored," and then practiced and repeated to form a new habit that works *for* you rather than *against* you.

Break Ineffective Patterns by Establishing Strong Routines or Habits
Routines are powerful habit formers and, if you identify a routine for the beginning of your trading session, you will create a support mechanism for optimal ability to perceive the reality of the market order flow. Of course, you might say, "I'm not willing to do all that. I'm ready to trade." Well, how

important is trading to you? Is it only for excitement and entertainment? If so, then why not just go to the casino?. Traders who are serious about being successful will gain enjoyment from masterful trading, using all of the tools and expertise at their disposal.

Consider revamping the way you start your day in an effort to completely snap you out of doing things 'the way you've always done them.' For many, this is the best way to make the necessary changes. Here is one powerful regimen that benefits mind, body and spirit and subsequently supports your capacity to accurately read what the market is saying.

- Start your day with exercise. Energize your system, oxygenate your bloodstream and get the cobwebs out of your brain and body. This does not have to be strenuous and, in fact, 30 minutes of calisthenics and stretching will bring great benefits. Believe me, if you haven't experienced the natural high that comes from a consistent period of first-thing-in-the-morning bodywork, then you're in for a treat. It is a thriving and revitalizing experience that leaves you glowing and confident for the day, ready to take on the challenges that await you.

- Try a meditative session to ground you in a relaxed and aligned state and help you become available, patient and focused with intention. By sitting still and focusing on your breath, you can ease any residual tension and center your system to be more proactive, resolute and attentive to what matters most.

- Eat a light breakfast of nutritious food, and drink juices and/or tea to maintain focus and mental strength. Eating is very important to incorporate and maintain proper minerals, vitamins and nutrients in the bloodstream for sugar balance and brain function. Your energy level must be high for prolonged and intense mental work, whether for an hour or several hours of market participation.

- Review your Plan and Trading Rules to keep them fresh in your mind. Keep them posted for easy reference while in the trading trenches. It is vital that you are familiar with your trading plan and rules intimately. You can't follow a rule you have forgotten.

- Do your homework, whatever supports your style and trading strategy. The point is to "do it."

- Go through your daily trading strategy "out loud." This has a way of flushing out distortions. Look at the charts you are planning to use. Identify the play you are going to make, and describe the rationale with entry, target, time frame and exit. You will be surprised at how the trade "sounds," and in fact, new perceptions of the trade may present themselves to either clarify and strengthen your confidence or shake you out of the dream that caused you to see something that wasn't really there.

- Then take a deep breath and enjoy becoming one with the price action and order flow. Remember, patience is a key ingredient to both seeing things as they are and waiting until the trade comes to you. Don't chase the trades.

States of Mind and Body

As the mood shifts into a pattern, it is followed by behavior that facilitates and illustrates the mood. Another important pattern interrupt is changing your physiology, for example:

- Change how you are sitting

- Take a moment to standup and literally get a different view

- Stretch and do deep breathing exercises along with a few deep knee bends

Changes in physiology can help to initiate a pattern interrupt and bring on a shift from an emotionally laden state of anxiety, fear, greed, and impulsivity to one of relaxation, focus, and centeredness. This is especially helpful when the markets get volatile and it's easy to get caught up in the ensuing excitement. That's the time to use a pattern interrupt and a physiological change. It's also an opportunity to use your Trading Rules as an anchor or reinforcement; keep them in front of you as a state stabilizer in troubled waters, to remain consistently purposeful, task oriented, and intentional about keeping rules.

Parts of the Self Speak Different Languages and See Different Things

Similar to the market, volatility is a direct reflection of the emerging emotions of the masses as they trade furiously, impulsively and, at times, capriciously and compulsively. By first attending to your own volatility, the market's messages can be apprehended.. As previously mentioned, the markets are organic. You climb into the skin of it and see yourself in its reflection. The successful trader "feels" the market, but does not get lost in those feelings. Losing the Ego attachments fosters the Zen of Trading by redefining the relationship to the trade. As in a business transaction with another human being, pure business with a neutral set of variables is a sterile process with the objective being the flow; that is, a detached interaction where (even when a profit is involved) we are not attempting to aggressively bleed the situation dry but come away having done well. We want to activate the "internal observer" by relaxing at every opportunity and creating the habit of "being present."

Activating the Internal Observer

Change physiology:

- Stand if sitting

- Straighten your back and body

- Take a good stretch

- Take a deep breath

- Engage parasympathetic of the Autonomic Nervous System – dilate blood vessels and increase oxygen to the brain and muscles slowing things down and initiating a Bentley's "Relaxation Response."

When ego investment and emotions rise, trading becomes a reflection of the ego (self-protection and self-promotion) and emotion. It creates a sort of delusion, and consequently, what we thought was a great trade was in reality a "fake out" or something that came from internal stimuli.

For example, after trading in a position on the Dow e-mini futures the YM, I violated my rule and failed to maintain a hard stop. It was on a day when the Dow lost over 300 points. The second rule I violated was to "think" that the ATR (Average True Range) had been breached and that, since its average daily range was violated, that it would "come back." The third rule I broke, after finally taking myself out of the trade for a significant loss, was to believe that increasing my position and essentially "doubling down" would bring me back to break-even. Now that was delusional thinking! My analysis was distorted by the emotional upheaval taking place after incurring the original loss. I did get back in the market only to lose more.

Rule-Governed Trading

Rule-governed trading offers a way to initiate, develop, and anchor a set of habits that help to significantly reduce the ego-driven tendencies. Before you begin your trading session, as a part of your routine, take your Emotional Temperature; that is, scan your feelings and general mood. Moods or emotional states have limiting languages and distort incoming data. In other words, moods and emotional states act as powerful filters. Take a deep breath and ask the questions:

- How do I feel?
- What is going on with me?
- What can I do to change right now?

Whether bored, anxious, excited, depressed or feeling any other difficult emotion, each presents it's own distraction/distortion factor. The ideal is to be on an even keel, open, available, fully present, relaxed and aligned. Try not to trade in difficult emotional states. It's best to incorporate a pattern interrupt if the mood is detected by the internal observer.

Your emotional arousal is correlated to the volatility in the market and your volatility or emotional swings can mean money swinging away from your pocket.

One of the states Trading Routines can promote is a Trading Zone, an internal state where you are prepared physically, emotionally and mentally to participate in the market. You are aligned correctly and what you see is reality. This capacity is developed through Trading Routines and various exercises that deepen personal awareness, sharpen focus, expand consciousness, and address improvables, for example: Meditation

- Emotional Freedom Technique

- Mental Rehearsal

- Reprogramming Tools

These are stand-alone exercises that, when practiced consistently, can help to develop the capacity for a "trading trance." These and other exercises and empowering techniques will be discussed later.

The importance of watching and waiting for the compelling reason to enter the trade cannot be overstated. Price patterns, volatility, sharp breakouts and breakdowns, pivot points, support and resistance are all derivatives of price action and demonstrate the market sentiments of other trades. Colin Wilson, in *New Pathways in Psychology,* said, "Nature has endowed human beings with a most adaptive capacity, the ability to learn new behaviors so well that they can perform them automatically without conscious effort. This is what happens when routines become habituated, the details of the behavior drop into the sub-conscious control where unconscious competence is achieved."

Four Fatal Fears

"Knowledge speaks, but wisdom listens." - Jimi Hendrix

If want greater success in your trading and investing, and in your life, what's really keeping you from getting those results? Perhaps you already know exactly what you want; what to do or stop doing to get the results you desire. Yet, interestingly, many continue to sabotage their own efforts and create the same negative results over and over again. The most important question we must ask, then, is why? When you first began to read this book, you may have felt sleepy. The need for sleep is powerful, and generally overrides other needs we may have. Regardless of how important this information is to you, your eyes were closing despite your best efforts to stay awake and concentrate. Humans seek comfort, and comfort encourages sleepiness.

What might have happened if you had sat straight up from your comfortable position? Possibly, your body would have realized it was not time to sleep, but time to act; to read this important information right now. So let's play an imagery game for a moment.

Find a comfortable position, and when you have finished reading these instructions, sit back, relax, close your eyes for a moment and take a deep breath. Visualize a calendar, and note that the dates on the calendar are moving ahead into the future... slowly at first, then faster and faster. Now visualize the calendar slowing down, and as it stops, you see it has moved 100 years into the future. Now, visualize the attic of an old house, where two children are going through an aged chest. These children are your great, great grandchildren. As they move through the items in the chest, they come across a funeral program with your picture on the front cover. They open the cover and begin to read your eulogy. What does that eulogy say about you? What kind of person were you?

What was your character? What did you accomplish? Were you liked and loved? Why? What did your friends and community have to say about you?

This can seem like a silly exercise at first. But it is actually quite important, so bear with the plan as we complete it.

Please write your answers to these questions on paper and set it aside to your right for a moment.

- On a separate piece of paper, visualize all the things you need on a daily basis to create success in your life; i.e., power, money, status, etc.. Write these things on a separate sheet of paper and place the paper to the left of you..

This list represents the things you value and tell yourself you "need."

Interestingly, the mind/brain is literal. Whatever you tell yourself you need, your mind will literally believe you need it to survive. For instance, you may have put down status and/or prestige as something you 'need' If these concepts have high value to you, they take on a "must have" quality. To illustrate this point, lets say that Jack's self-esteem and value as a person is tied up in his job. Then, God forbid, he loses his job for some reason. Jack, in all likelihood, will be devastated. He may be lost, confused and unable to rebound from his unfortunate circumstances, simply because he has allowed his job to grossly narrow his perception of himself. When the job fails, so does Jack. His "survival" as a human being is tied to this transient relationship. He has convinced himself that, in order to survive, he must "have" and "keep" *this* job.

When viewed more closely, there are only four things we "must" have in order to survive:

- Air

- Water

- Food

- Shelter

That's all we really 'need'. But as soon as you tell yourself you need one of those other items, your mind goes into survival mode. If you've even felt sure that if you didn't get a certain car, a promotion, a job, or a house you wanted, or did not make money on a certain trade, that something very bad was going to happen—you'll fail, be a loser, an outcast, rejected, and deep down it feels like you'll die...you have been operating in survival mode. Attempting to make wise long term decisions when those capabilities are skewed by survival mode thinking is short term...almost childish. And the long term consequences can be devastating.

Fritz Kunkel, noted author, stated there are basically 4 fatal fears he discovered in western civilization. These fears have kept human beings from creating the results they want in their lives, just like the results that you identified a few moments ago. If you're like most folks, those results have nothing to do with jobs, promotions, money, cars, or houses. In fact, it's arguable that no one at the end of his or her life has ever said, "I wish I had spent more time at the office." These fears are fatal, not to your life, but to those precious things you said you wanted your life to mean in the end. No, these fears are not those associated with violence, tragic accidents or footsteps in a dark alley. We need this kind of fear; it is a normal part of life brought about by the internal default mechanism called Fight or Flight. The fear we are talking about are ego-driven fears or, to put it more simply, false evidence appearing real. We confront theses fears every day—even though we are not fully aware at that time we are operating from a fear-based position.

Fear stems from the threat of loss or the perception of a need that, if left unfulfilled, would cause a threat to personal well-being and self esteem. For example, consider the fear of failure. What kind of need causes one to fear failure? The need for success or the need to win. Do you see how this works? As soon as I say to myself, *"In order to be an OK person, in order to feel good about myself in the world, I need to be successful, and I need to be seen as a winner"*, fear of failure begins to take control over my decisions . I may not be likely to try things where I can't guarantee my success. At least not in public. If you sing in the shower and fantasize about being a professional singer, and yet would rather have a stick in the eye than actually stand in front of people and raise a joyful noise, you've just experienced the fear of success.

Let's look at those other fatal fears. How about fear of rejection? This is nothing more than the need to be loved and accepted. Emotional Discomfort, including fear of embarrassment, fear of humiliation, fear of looking silly, fear of intimacy, fear of conflict, and the fear of being vulnerable is driven by the need for emotional safety or, as they say today, 'staying in your comfort zone'. The need to be right or the fear of being wrong is an overwhelming need to have all the answers.

Do any of these look familiar? No doubt, since they are all central to human behavior. How often do they appear in your life? Let's look again at those two sheets of paper. Let's call the one on the left *'Playing not to lose'* (i.e., driven by fear). Put that title at the top of this list. Let's call the one on the right *'Playing to win'* (i.e., driven by courage). Place this title at the top of the right sheet of paper. Looking at the list on the left, consider these the prizes we are playing for at the cost of those items on the right- - those items we value so much and want our lifelong legacy to reflect. Items on the left sheet are the "actual" things that are most important; things like , goals, rewards, awards, cars, houses, boats, jewelry, clothes, and money that we think we must have. In other words, the unconscious conversation may go something like this: *I will be seen as a winner and I'll avoid looking like a failure if I drive a fancy car, live in a big house, have power and prestige, etc.* I am not saying it is wrong to want and enjoy nice things in life; however, it is the underlying intention that is important. Are you craving them as status or do you simply enjoy them?

You see, "winning" and "success" are really not as important as "looking" like a winner or looking successful. If this were not true, you would never catch people doing things like cheating, buying things they can't afford, or going deep into debt to get these "things". And, the same thing holds true about being right! In fact, ask yourself this question: Is it more important for people to be right or to have others *think* they are right? If you are married, have you ever argued with your spouse (the person you deeply love more than anyone in the world, with maybe the exception of your children) and suddenly realized with absolute clarity that YOU ARE WRONG.. and yet you keep on arguing? Winning the argument at that moment...being right... became more important than your love for your wife, your feelings for your children, or any other 'need'. The legal system reflects this as well; justice seems less important than presenting the better argument (even when it involves someone's life). Since the advent of DNA testing, hundreds of death row inmates have been proven wrongly incarcerated and were released. . Yet, on the day they were pronounced guilty, the prosecution, the judge and the jury knew they were *right*. Many things in life can be yours if you excel at the *playing not to lose* game, or PNTL.

What about the Right List of items, items you want to be recognized for or want to accomplish before you die? This would be the *playing to win* or the PTW list. For most of you, theses look very different. These are the things you *said* you really wanted, things so important that you want to be remembered for them. They are not fear-driven. They are adventure and love-driven. You hear a lot in business these days about learning organizations, about growth and development. Those things live over there in the Right List.

Which list do you want to live on? How many times, despite your best intentions, have you found yourself on the left, living in the Four Fatal Fears?

If you've ever gambled, at casinos in Las Vegas, you know the casinos seldom actually play. Every time you put your money on the poker table, the house gets a percentage. If I'm the House, I don't care whether Tony wins or Margaret wins, because I've already got my share. Let's call the house Life. And let's call Life's share of the pot time. Every day that passes, the House takes minutes, weeks, months, and years. In the end, the House gets it all. You may feel like you will live forever, but no one does. This can be illustrated easily by taking a line like this:

0 _____ end-of-your-life.

The normal life expectancy is somewhere around 85 years today. If you are 25, you have already lived almost a third of your life. If you are 40 you have lived almost half of your life. For the old timers, 50 or more, you've lived 60% or more. But, we don't live our lives as though it is running out; we live as though time has no relevance, as though we have an unlimited supply. At the age of 54, my father he was informed he had "terminal" cancer. that the doctor said unequivocally that he "would" die. That's very sad for anyone who has this experience. But the fact is, we all 'will' die. As time ticks by, we may remain oblivious, but time does not stop and the House will get their ante.

If you choose to play at the PNTL table, consider these things:

- You win the possibility of succeeding or getting what you say you want and avoiding failure

- You win the possibility of being right and avoiding being wrong

- You have the possibility of having the appearance of acceptance, and avoiding rejection

- You have the possibility of having emotional comfort and avoiding emotional discomfort.

But there are no guarantees, of course, because this is gambling. Every single time you play a hand at either one of the tables, you are betting on the results of your life and you have given your initial ante, *your time*. The same hand is being dealt on your right at the PTW table. Again, you're gambling and nothing is guaranteed. Of every hand that's dealt, you're saying, "I'm betting that I can get growth and joy in my life. Out of every hand, I'm betting that I can have greater understanding, great relationships, and live my life with integrity." So with every hand, you're making a decision that this is what you want to play for, PLAYING TO WIN or PLAYING NOT TO LOSE.

So here's the catch. Am I saying these two are mutually exclusive, that you can't have both in your life? Yes and no, and let me show you why. You can say "I want to experience the growth and fulfillment of a *play to win* life and, by the way, it's also important to me to be seen as a winner and have acceptance." And most of us come from that place. But when the rubber hits the road, when you get that event in your life that's very difficult, and you have to make a choice, that's when you can't play both games at the same time.

If you're playing at the PTW table, you may be faced with a choice between great relationships and being right. Your play will be to behave in a way that enhances your relationships with courage and honesty, engaging in the difficult conversations and risking discomfort for the sake of the relationship. If you're playing on the PNTL table, and you are faced with a choice between a great relationship and being right, what do you think you'll choose? PTW players would rather be right. Or what about never allowing yourself into situations where you might be embarrassed, show vulnerability, look foolish or act silly,? So you bet on the PNTL side.

The choice between tables, PNTL, or PTW is up to each of us, and it is a choice for LIFE. The naturalist Robert Ingersoll and the great writer Helen Keller both observed that, in nature, there are no rewards or punishments, just consequences. When we choose to avoid the FFF's, we guarantee ourselves that when we come to those dozen choice-points a day, we are going to choose the path of safety and not growth. When we consistently choose—day in and day out—the path of safety and defense, it becomes more than a series of choices. The consequence is that playing not to lose becomes a life strategy, a complete plan for how we run our lives and how we want it all to turn out.

Controlling Your Emotions With Your Mind

"If you can imagine it, you can achieve it; if you can dream it, you can become it." - William Arthur Ward

Getting control of your emotions is a tough task at best. So it is helpful to know why it can be so difficult and why it is important to 'get a grip' on what we feel.

The Strongest Mental Models Are Created in Early Childhood

Childhood emotional traumas, wounds, and scars create the crux of our MAPs and paradigms. How we see the world is influenced by the way we bonded with our parents/family in the first 3 to 5 years of life. A secure bond or attachment means a nurturing upbringing, complete with plenty of affection and limits, as well as room to explore. A secure attachment is one of two main constructs that form the foundation of our MAPs. The remaining types of attachments all fall under the "insecure" topic and indicate that your caregivers/parents/family were erratic, inconsistent, withheld love and affection and may have even been abusive. These two bonding strategies are formed by our earliest relationships. If those relationships were good, our outlook is mostly positive; if painful, then our outlook is likely more negative. These emotions continue to play out over and over again, triggered by associations and reminders of the past or by strong emotions such as anxiety and fear that activate internal states that cascade a plethora of thoughts, images and additional emotions. Trading time machines can happen at any moment when the relationship with the market goes sour and can activate feelings of envy, jealousy, betrayal, abandonment, anger, guilt, desperation and depression. At these times, the trader is caught in a time warp where old image tapes begin to play and the trader is seemingly held captive in the clutches of those old recordings. To get out of the abyss brought on by the cascade of chemicals that originally encoded these states, the resources of the right brain—where these emotions are lodged and largely held unexpressed to the conscious mind—must be flushed out and purged by shedding light on these dark spaces through right brain mediated exercises. Trading becomes a mirror for life's relationships. When money is at stake through immediate pleasure-pain dichotomies of trading, old learned limitation strategies are activated. State bound memory learning and behaviors formed out of old traumas create patterns of coping that, in many instances, are maladaptive defenses that work against the trader. These patterns of thinking and doing emerge from learned limitations and belief systems. In order to override these patterns, they must first be interrupted, and the distortions created by the original beliefs must be shown to be the illusions that they are.

When psychological trauma takes place, the system mobilizes to defend against both the event recurring and the thoughts and emotions associated with it. It's an attempt to defend against fear, depression, and emotional pain. Maladaptive coping strategies are designed by the unconscious to help, but this ends up causing immobility, overcompensation and a mixed bag of less than positive or neutral emotions. In fact, it can get quite complex. For example, not only can there be fear, but the system can develop fear of the fear; not only is there stress from the event, but the system can develop stress of the stress. This fear of the fear can be illustrated by the way "triggers" work. Triggers are cues in our internal or external environment that trigger a response. If you had an abusive father who yelled at you and said you were incompetent and would never amount to anything, you might be surprised how these old tapes can affect the trade. In the heat of a trade, if the price action goes against you significantly, your subconscious might replay those old tapes, prompting a severe anxiety reaction accompanied by the dread and fear of taking risk. Later, in another similar trade, you may remember the anxiety, fear and self-loathing you felt before and, by just considering the same type of trade, you may experience a fear of having those feelings again. When we "split" from our calm, normal, focused self to an anxious or agitated state, the results can cause impulsivity and compulsivity, methods used to defend against the emotions elicited by the triggers. Embrace the anxiety, greed, fear, anger, frustration, guilt, shame, or procrastination. At this point you can use the Stop, Challenge and Choose exercise to examine how you feel about the event. Use this opportunity to write in your thought journal and bring yourself closer to awareness the story you are telling. Within those emotions lie the treasures of your growth. We can't change what we can't face.

This is an opportunity to provide for your own intervention. Identify yourself as the client and teach her/him the importance of establishing behavioral strategies to trigger and reframe old paradigms and mental models of the problem and issues. Reframing is a powerful tool that creates a turnaround context for an ineffective model. For instance, a failure does not mean that you're incompetent. Everyone fails. Rather, it means that you've had another opportunity to learn. Most successful traders will tell you that they lost many times and blew up several accounts before they acquired the knowledge, experience, and set of effective habits that took them to success. Get a new set of lenses with which to "see" the issues. Lenses are ground out through identifying and challenging the mythology of your MAPs. Focus on your clients' strengths and embellish them. If you haven't already, make a list of your strengths and put them in the service of your goals, where one important goal is the creation of a new model for the client to emulate. It's better to identify one new pattern and make it a habit than to try many patterns intermittently.

Mardi Horowitz, a trauma researcher, wrote about what he calls mastery, which is a salient point to make here. He espoused the importance of "working through" the issue when difficult emotions arise. This process of "working through" is what we have been discussing. It involves confronting, increasing awareness, reframing, and establishing behavioral strategies. Or, you can continue to do what you have been doing and get the same results you have been getting. What we want to achieve is going from unconscious incompetence to conscious competence and finally to unconscious competence, that is, from *not knowing that we don't know* to *knowing that we know* and having to think about it, and finally having our knowledge and ability ease into habituation and skill without having to think about it.

Donald Michenbaum's language of healing works well as a way to positively self-talk when dealing with identified instances of impulsivity and compulsivity. It is designed to help you "write yourself a new narrative for effective trading results." Positive self-talk is initiating the coach within. Aside from helping to maintain focus, it also engages the parasympathetic nervous system (which calms and relaxes the body) and redirects attention from the distractions of negative and counterproductive thinking and emotions to those that empower and support goal oriented decisions. What is important is to construct affirmative statements on your ability to cope and to demonstrate resilience and courage in the face of trades that have gone against you and drawdowns. For instance:

- You demonstrate the ability to reframe events from failures to lessons.

- You are able to see your trade and strategy through a new set of lenses.

- You resist the temptation of feeling fear, greed, self-repudiation, self-loathing, and self-hate, anger and wishful thinking that distract you from your plan and strategy.

- You author your plan and keep your rules.

- You demonstrate the ability to maintain proactive and effective routines.

- You make choices based upon reality.

- You realize that you have boundless opportunities to trade.

- You decide to develop a more comfortable relationship with yourself.

- You create and maintain a strong purpose and mission for your trading business.

- You leave behind those things that should be left behind.

- You take initiative to continue to update and follow your rules.

- You take back your power when you feel an urge to violate your rules.

- You get rid of the excess baggage of ineffective programs.

- You liberate your trading from the lack and limited thinking.

- You notice a calmer more patient you

- You catch yourself entering and exiting your trade exactly according to your pre-targeted plan.

- You realized many of your strengths, powers and capacities by keeping your commitment to your rules.

- You develop a winning strategy.

- You recognize that the most important point is not whether or not you made a profit, but whether you kept your rules.

The Power of Altered States of Consciousness

Trading in the zone, a phrase coined by Brett Steenbarger, PhD., in his book "The Psychology of Trading", means shifting into an altered state of consciousness. Getting into the flow is another way to say it as well. Essentially, we are talking about raising our consciousness to the meta-level; in other words, becoming focused and initiating an alpha wave. An alpha state is an extremely relaxed and highly productive state of mind that is conducive to being in the flow. Below are brief descriptions of the four brain wave ranges.

- The *beta* - about 13 to 40 or so cycles per second on the Hertz scale, a normal waking state where we spend most of our time and go through mundane mental machinations of everyday life.

- The *alpha*, about 8 to 13 cycles per second on the Hz scale, a dissociative inter-communicative state, where we can lose sense of time.

- The *theta*, about 4.5 to 8 cycles per second, an associative intra-communicative state often associated with REM sleep and day or night dreaming when the subconscious uses images and symbols to communicate with the conscious.

- The *delta*, a deep dreamless sleep state with a very slow brain wave. 0.4 to about 4.5 cycles per second on the Hertz scale.

When you are daydreaming, or half asleep, or in the "flow", you are in an altered state. Using altered states of consciousness is like tuning into different frequencies or vibrations that correspond to internal states.; for example, using self-hypnosis to bring on the state of relaxation and calm coupled with the state of alertness and focus, and with the state of confidence and optimism, or using a technology called binaural signals that, when listened to, balance the left and right brains in a way that supports clarity and diminishes distortion.

Using meditation to expand the consciousness and ability of the mind to attune to subtle changes in information or data flow is called The "dial of consciousness", used to tune into different levels of consciousness to increase flexibility of receptivity to new information (Brett Stentenbarger). It also involves a context shift, moving to a new physiological structure and stance: changes in movement, posture, breathing, standing, changing behavior by changing context.

"It is not the critic who counts; not the man who points out how the strong man stumbles, or where the doer of deeds could have done them better. The credit belongs to the man who is actually in the arena, whose face is marred by dust and sweat and blood, who strives valiantly; who errs and comes short again and again; because there is not effort without error and shortcomings; but who does actually strive to do the deed; who knows the great enthusiasm, the great devotion, who spends himself in a worthy cause, who at the best knows in the end the triumph of high achievement and who at the worst, if he fails, at least he fails while daring greatly. So that his place shall never be with those cold and timid souls who know neither victory nor defeat." - Theodore Roosevelt

Reframing: The Power of Controlled Perception

An important trading lesson is that of *reframing* the concept of loss and learning to accept it routinely. Reframing is an initiative that involves shifting thinking around a particular concept so that the emphasis changes from negative to positive, from constriction to expansion, from weak to empowering, from non-supportive to supportive.

An example of reframing:

Concept: "My losses are eating up all of my money."

The reframe: "Losses are the cost of doing business and are part of trading," or "I like losses, for every small loss gets me closer to a big win."

Reframing is a technique in Neuro-Linguistic Programming (NLP) where an undesirable behavior or trait is transformed into a positive premise or intention. Alternatives to satisfy the positive intent are found, followed by negotiations with (parts of) self to resolve conflict, check for ecology, and to implement the new behavior. Reframing can also be used in NLP to describe changing the context or representation of a problem. More precisely, one of the most effective techniques for achieving almost any desired change in NLP is the "six step reframe."

The 6-step Reframe

1) Identify the pattern (X) to be changed; example, doubling down when in a losing position. It can be any behavior that you either want to discontinue or want to start.

2) Establish communication with the part of yourself that is responsible for the pattern. This is founded on the active assumption that all aspects of yourself are valuable parts. In other words, these parts are predicated on achieving a goal for the system; for instance protection and safety. Fear of success can have an underlying premise that actually is initiated to "protect" you from the potential pain of rejection when the internal myth of being undeserving is challenged.

2a) The important question is: Will the part of me that runs pattern X communicate with me in consciousness?

2b) Establish a "yes-no" meaning of the signal. This might be a tangible feeling coming from anywhere in the system—your muscles getting tense, your stomach getting fluttery, etc. Declare the following: "If this feeling means yes, then increase this sensation." Actually, any of the kinesthetic, visual or sound-related experiences would be very good vehicles to look for when communicating with the unconscious. Of course, the conscious cannot choose which communication conduit will work. That would be like answering for the other person in a conversation, until they say something you don't know.

3) Distinguish between the behavior, pattern X, and the intention of the part that is responsible for the behavior.

3a) Ask the question "Would you be willing to let me know in consciousness what you are trying to do for me by pattern X?" After asking, then just as before, you want to remain open to the sensation that already has begun, only a diminishing or an increasing of that sensation.

3b) If you get a "yes" response, ask the part to go ahead and communicate its intention.

3c) Is that intention acceptable to consciousness? Once the intention of the part causing the behavior has been discovered, and there is conscious understanding, it is important that the specific method it uses to creatively replace the behavior is acceptable to you (the conscious). You may not like the way it goes about accomplishing pattern X, but do you agree that the intention is something you want to have a part do for you as a person? When that happens, there is congruency between the intention of the unconscious part and the appreciation of the conscious.

4) Create new alternative behaviors to satisfy the intention. At the unconscious level, the part that runs pattern X communicates its intention to the creative part, and selects from the alternatives that the creative part generates. Each time it selects an alternative, it gives the "yes" signal. You could ask yourself if you have a "creative part", part of all normal beings due to the inherent necessity of creativity in order to survive and thrive in the world. Then, go inside and ask your creative part if it would be willing to undertake the following task: go to the unconscious level (the part that runs pattern X) and find out what that part is trying to do for you. Then have it create alternative ways by which this part of you can accomplish this intention. It may create hundreds of ways to get that outcome, and it's to be quite random and irresponsible in this. The part of you that is running pattern X will evaluate which of those ways it believes are more effective than pattern X in getting what it's been trying to get for you. It is to select 3 ways that it believes will work at least as effectively as the pattern of behavior it's been using up to now. After three choices have been identified, check to see that those three are acceptable to the part running pattern X. If it is not then have the creative part continue again until you get 3 acceptable signals or choices.

5) Ask the part: "Are you willing to take responsibility for generating the three new alternatives in the appropriate context, since you have three ways that are more effective than the old pattern X?" You're making sure those new choices actually occur in your new behavior.

6) Ecological check. "Is there any other part of me that objects to the three new alternatives?" If there is a "yes' response, recycle to step 2 above. This step is what makes this model for change really elegant. The ecological check is our explicit recognition that you are a really complex and balanced organism. It takes into account all the repercussions in other parts of your experience and behavior that would be foolhardy.

In psychotherapy, after irrational beliefs have been identified, the therapist will often work with the client by challenging negative thoughts on the basis of evidence, reframing experiences in a more realistic or positive light. This can help clients to develop more rational beliefs and healthy coping strategies. Reframing occurs in life regardless of NLP, and is a common way that meanings get created, either deliberately or by chance. For instance, Jamie does not like to be criticized and tends to get angry at unsolicited advise. Her thoughts have been: "This person is trying to control me." Jack, a friend and fellow trader, is someone Jamie respects and admires. Jamie recently had a deep drawdown in her account due to making similar mistakes in her technical analysis. In a conversation with Jack, she did something that she does not normally do, out of frustration; she explained her strategy to Jack. Immediately, he noticed the trouble, but rather than blurt it out, he gently questioned her about her strategy and slowly and deliberately uncovered from Jamie her underlying misconceptions that led her to misinterpret the charts. Due to Jack's calm and respectful approach, Jamie was able to remain focused on the process and therefore could "hear" Jack. She got it and the interaction greatly helped her clarity about the charts. As a result, she was able to reframe the thought: "People who give criticism are trying to control me which drove the feeling of irritation and anger to a new thought – some people are open to help and are willing to support me." This is an example of how reframes can happen in everyday life.

Filters: The Lenses Through Which We See the World

MAPs and paradigm programming also involve how we perceive the world; in other words, the lenses we use to "filter" information. There are as many ways to filter data coming into our brain/mind for processing as there are people. And, it's important to understand some of the more general ways that filters work. In this way, we will be able to promote changing "what" we do through "how" we do it. Doing things differently as a result of seeing and experiencing things differently is what we are talking about.

Let's look at some of them and then we will apply them:

Associated/Disassociated Filters

Associated filters are distinguished by your being attached to an experience as imagining being "in" your body. Think about one of your most recent trades, whether positive or negative. If you are able to experience it again as if you were there by *hearing* the sounds from your ears, *seeing* the charts through your eyes, *touching* the keys of your computer with your fingers, and *feeling* the emotions again that you felt at the time while watching that price action either go with you or against you, you are filtering the event in an *associated* way. You are in your body. If on the other hand you saw yourself as though you were an *outside* observer and experienced yourself as someone else, then you are said to be *dissociated*.

Why is this important? Take a moment to think about your trading room as you are in it. Notice the placement of the furniture, your computer and other tools. Also, notice the colors and lighting. As you become more aware of the space, notice if there are sounds, and if so, distinguish what they are: loud, soft, pleasant, annoying. As you experience yourself in this space, you can become aware of your body, feel its textures and pressure, sense the parts of you that are touching the furniture or the ground, feel the temperature of the room. Is it warm or chilled? Allow yourself to notice smells or tastes; perhaps you eat lunch or a snack at your desk from time to time. As you are doing this, pay attention to any emotions, tensions, excitement, etc. and to the location in your body. What you are doing is experiencing an *associated* state.

Now, step back and view the same scene as though you were someone else looking at you. See yourself in your office and notice everything "external" to your body, sounds and sights. See the whole you and be aware of how the "whole" you looks and sounds. This is a *dissociated* state. It is detached from your inner experience.

The ability to associate or dissociate is a fundamental skill, with each state offering different benefits in order to at times experience feelings, emotions, and events as though you were there in an associated fashion, or to distance yourself from unpleasant, or traumatic situations.

With difficult incidents of our past sapping our strength and compromising our resolve, it is not only helpful but also empowering to be able to dissociate and distance ourselves from the event(s). Additionally, we can manipulate the filter by exaggerating the distance through increasing or decreasing the modality, that is, what we see, hear, feel, taste, smell, and touch. I'll say more about this later, but it is extremely important to helping ameliorate both old, nagging traumas and memories of distant and near past events that can significantly detract from our trading discipline and focus. Conversely, uplifting and intensely supportive visions of the future can be paced more strongly by associating with the experience and feeling, touching, tasting, smelling and seeing what it will be like when it is achieved. And, in this instance, dissociation can be used as well to "see" and otherwise experience yourself in the future reality. And here's something you probably didn't know: with regard to stress and trauma, those that relive the memories in an associated way add to their stress and experience longer lasting and more intensely because they inflict the intensity of the event(s) as though it were happening again and again. Those with the lowest levels of stress are able to dissociate and detach from the experience.

Big Picture/Detail Filters

Some traders are driven by Fundamentals and some have an eye for Technical Analysis. Both of these orientations are valid and either offer controversy for hard liners. Within these ranks, there are those that look for the macro picture and are drawn to it. Macro-oriented or big picture traders are for the most part swing traders (in the trade for two or more weeks) and long-term traders (in for weeks to months). They prefer to analyze longer-term economic trends and look at charts that have longer-term data. Detail oriented individuals or micro-data traders often prefer intra-day to short term (days to a couple of weeks time frame). They are looking for the quick pop. Obviously, neither of these filters is wrong. It depends on your preference. However, it is important that you be aware your filter for information will impact upon what you see and how you see it.

Past/Present/ Future Filters

Some people have a penchant for the past. Some people are enamored with back testing, and many will tell you that back testing will only tell you what the price action did in the past under those circumstances. Others prefer to be in the present, and still there are those that live in the future. For instance, questions like: What's for dinner? How long until we get home? What's next on the agenda? all look to the future. There is no right or wrong, good or bad, but it does present a filter for how we communicate with ourselves regarding what we see and how we process the information.

Internal/External Filters

Internally-referenced people rely on their feelings, thoughts, images and voices as evidence of being correct, appropriate or being fulfilled. *Externally*-referenced people look to evidence outside of themselves for validation of their opinions and ideas. Your preference will play a big role in the way that you trade. If you are externally referenced, you are more susceptible to the influence of the "experts" and prone to heed the opinions of others while in a trade. People who are independent in style are usually internally referenced. They may listen to the opinions of others but rarely do they depend on them for validation of their own proclivities. When they have analyzed a trade, they feel confident. Conversely, people who are more driven by an external perspective will place a substantive portion of their confidence in what the pundits have to say. Again, the important thing is to be aware of how you think, embrace reality and find a balance that honors your own analytic abilities, but appreciates outside resources as beneficial modes of additional information.

Towards/Away From Filters

If you envision a goal, personal or professional, short or long term, it's important to be aware of how you are thinking about the goal. Are you envisioning what it would be like to have the goal (how it feels, looks, smells, tastes, and sounds)? Or are you inundated by all the ways that it might fail and haunted by what that failure will feel, look, smell, taste and sound like? This is a very important filter to be aware of. A *towards* filter engages your subconscious, especially if it is in a sensory rich fashion, and the subconscious relates to it as though it were real. Those who have this filter are much more likely to attract and achieve their goal. Those who think of (especially in a sensory rich way by feeling, seeing, smelling, tasting, and hearing) what they don't want are more likely to attract or achieve just that. This is especially important when putting your purpose, mission, goals, and profit objectives together. Remember, in the words of comic Flip Wilson "What you see is what you get."

Hypnotic Language – It's Not What You Say But How You Say It

"Argue for your limitations, and sure enough they're yours." - Richard Bach

Language is powerful, to say the least. Words have launched wars, motivated minions, soothed sensibilities and birthed nations. Language is one of the principle ways we learn and are programmed. This programming can take place through engaging the subconscious via altered states of consciousness, as in hypnosis and trance states. Language can be described as thought precipitates; that is, codified and structured sounds that are formed by and emanate from thought. We define ourselves by the language we use. Our self-concept is detailed by the story we tell ourselves and share with others. Our interpretations of the world depend upon the words we choose to describe it. Additionally, the questions we ask contain the assumptions or our MAPs and paradigms of the world. These MAPs, mental models and paradigms are largely formed by events that were first codified by word descriptions, chosen by either ourselves or by others as a response to interpretations of events. Also, these events, especially in our young years, not only involved interpretations but also deep-seated emotions that memorialized the learning and the description of that learning of the event. In response to an abusive event, it is much different if a 4-year-old says, "It's my fault. I am bad," as opposed to, "It's not my fault." It is critically important to be skillful in language, not just for the obvious reasons, but also to support our own efforts. Consider the following. We can choose language that is in line with the outcomes we want to achieve. "We can do this if we all work together and pull our own weight." We can create space in our language for others to draw on their own resources rather than relying on us for answers, helping to build self-esteem and confidence as in, "I wonder how you will creatively come up with just the right solution to this issue?" We can respect other unique interpretations of a situation, especially when we do not know the context. For instance, "Oh, that's interesting. I seem to see it differently, so please help me understand how you reached that conclusion."

We are programming others and ourselves most of the time using language. The use of language is essential in directing a person's experience and focus of attention. One of the most revered teachers and masters of the use of language as a tool for change was Dr. Milton Erickson, often thought to be the grandfather of clinical hypnosis in the U.S. Dr. Erickson was a psychiatrist who, after being struck with polio at 17, developed a deep ability to use the creative resources of his unconscious, first to address his own health and later with patients after he became a psychiatrist. He is noted for his often unconventional approach to psychotherapy, such as described in the book *Uncommon Therapy*, by Jay Haley, and the book *Hypnotherapy: An Exploratory Casebook,* by Milton H. Erickson and Ernest L. Rossi (1979, New York: Irvington Publishers, Inc.) He is also known for his extensive use of therapeutic metaphor and story, as well as hypnosis. Additionally, he coined the term "Brief Therapy" for his approach of addressing therapeutic changes in relatively few sessions. He is revered for his conceptualization of the unconscious as highly separate from the conscious mind, with its own awareness, interests, responses, and learnings.

For Erickson, the unconscious mind was creative, solution-generating, and often positive. Furthermore, he is known for his ability to utilize anything about a patient to help them change, including their beliefs, favorite words, cultural background, personal history, or even their neurotic habits. And, he is known for his influence on Neuro-Linguistic Programming (NLP), which was ,in part, based upon his working methods. The Milton Model, named after Milton

Erickson, lists the key parts of speech and key patterns that are useful in subtly and effectively directing another person's line of thinking. Useful in sales, therapy, family relations and in gaining rapport in general, the principles of the Milton Model basically state that larger chunks (more general use of language) can lead to more rapport, which smaller chunks, (more specific language) is more limiting and has a greater chance of excluding concepts from a person's experience. This kind of "language" can be of great importance when describing and defining our own experience as we talk to ourselves. The following is a list of language techniques that can be extremely helpful in structuring your perspective; that is, how you "see", which impacts greatly upon what and how you "do."

Nominalizations

To nominalize something means to make a noun out of something intangible that doesn't exist in a concrete sense (in NLP, it is said that any noun you can't put in a wheelbarrow is a nominalization). If I were to say, "You know you can feel confident about some learnings from last weekend", learnings is an example of a nominalization. In this example, the process of learning something is turned into a noun: learnings. Being happy becomes happiness, being curious becomes curiosity and being depressed becomes depression. A state like depression becomes an enormous and sometimes insurmountable, overwhelming state of being; for example, whereas being depressed to most people is more likely to imply a state that has a beginning, and more importantly an end. A block is something much more insurmountable than something that is merely blocking your progress. As an example, consider the following: "So close your eyes and think for a moment about a recent learning, one that may have given you much surprise and enjoyment." Notice in the previous sentence the speaker doesn't say how or where, but allows the listener to fill in with his or her own details.

Unspecified Nouns and Verbs

"People can learn to trade easily under hypnosis." There are a few things in this sentence that are not clear: Which people? And how can they learn to trade easily? When phrases like these are used, the listener is forced to use his or her imagination to fill in the who's and how's. Again, these types of phrases are useful for pacing and leading when the speaker, by becoming too specific, could mismatch the listener and break rapport or minimize influence.

"So take a moment and enjoy remembering some of the things you learned and did at the seminar."

What were your thoughts after hearing that sentence? Did you have a specific representation, (visual, kinesthetic, or auditory)?

Unspecified Referential Indices

Unspecified referential indices are nouns that don't refer to something specific, i.e., "*This* is much easier to learn than it looks at first." *This* doesn't really tell us what it refers to. We guess and make an internal decision about the topic of the sentence. "*People* can relax and trade well." We need to guess which *people*.

Unspecified verbs and adverbs also let us fill in with our own experience. For instance, without referring to price action and the charts specifically, we might say, "*This* is much easier to learn than it looks at first." "*It* is much easier to follow as it ticks up and down." "*People* can relax." We don't know how it is easier to follow your rules, or how it looks at first. Nor do we know how successful traders relax and manage their money, nor how they can do it. But we can imagine how.

Commentary adjectives and adverbs are a way that we can lead people to easily accept our presuppositions. "How soon will you be *pleasantly* surprised by *easily* remembering and using the tools you have learned about money management and following your rules?"

Use of the comparable "And As" are another type of connectors that place two powerful adverb phrases together: "If anyone can follow the price action as *methodically and as successfully as you do*, they must be extremely motivated and thorough."

Semantic Ill-Formedness
Lost Performatives. It's important to know about these structures, because it's often necessary to deliver presuppositions indirectly. These types of phrases contain at least one judgment or evaluation of which we can't identify the source. For instance:

- It's important to learn language patterns.
- It's essential to enjoy exercising successful money management.
- It's important that we follow our rules.

The speaker doesn't state exactly who thinks these things are good, necessary or important.

Conversational Postulates are requests for action or information masquerading as yes/no questions.

- "Can you tell me what time it is?"

- "Do you know what today's date is?"

- "Can you lend me a pen?"

- "Can you go into a trance easily?"

- "Can you follow your rules easily?"

Presuppositions are ways of indirectly getting agreement from a listener. There are several types of presuppositions:

- Existence: "She saw the ice cream in the freezer." "He saw the journal log sitting next to his computer screen." Implies is, was, may be.

- Time: Before, after, during, continue, yet, already, begin, stop, start, still, while, since, as, and when. "You may hear noises in the room while you are entering a state of deep relaxation." " You may see the price action while you calculate targets and stops."

- Ordinals: These assume action will be taken, the question is, in what order, 1st, 2nd, 3rd, etc. "Do you want to take a deep breath or would you like to settle down into your chair first?" "Do you want to take a deep breath and identify your strategy for this trade first, and then identify your target price and stops second?"

The use of "or": "Would you prefer a silk blouse *or* one in cotton?" This presupposes that the listener wants a blouse. The question is which. This form of language is often heard in sales closing and can be quite powerful. "Would you like to follow a discretionary trading strategy while practicing tight money management *or* would you prefer to system trading strategy with your rules programmed in and position sizing already established?" This presupposes that you actually will follow rules and use appropriate money management however you trade or invest.

Awareness: In this technique the listener is prompted to assume the statement is true, all that may be questioned is whether the listener is aware. *"Have you realized* how common it is to be in a trance?" *"Have you noticed* how often you go into a trance, even by yourself?" *"Did you realize that* you can list and follow your rules quite effectively?" "Did you recognize how easily and how effectively money management can work for you, in every trade?"

Adverbs and Adjectives: Another presupposition refers to something that is going to happen. The issue is how will the experience be?

- "What have you enjoyed the most about practicing successful money management?"

- "Are you excited about making this trade while following all of your rules?"

- "How easily can you set your stops?"

- "Fortunately we have plenty of opportunity to practice powerful position sizing."

Other Patterns

Embedded Suggestions are suggestions or directives buried within a larger sentence. They allow the speaker to ask more subtly and in a way that the listener can respond sometimes without consciously knowing he or she has been asked. (We do this all the time without realizing it).

- "I don't know how soon you'll *feel better.*"

- "You can *learn* these patterns *easily.*"

- "I wonder how quickly you will *incorporate following your rules in all your trading.*"

Negative Commands use the inability of your unconscious to comprehend language constructions that use negatives (No, Not, Don't, etc.). For instance, if someone were to say, "Don't think about pink elephants," what happens? Using negative commands can be thought of as sending subliminal messages to the brain. Since the unconscious cannot process the negative, only the positive message registers.

- "*Don't relax* too quickly when you sit in front of your computer screen."

- "It's important that you *don't practice powerful money management* any sooner than you feel comfortable doing so."

- "Don't go into a trance too soon . . ."

Ambiguity: When words have double meaning, the unconscious mind must process all meanings. Words like down, left, duck, hand, back all have double meanings. Then there are words that are spelled differently and pronounced the same. Hear/here, your/you're, nose/knows are examples. These can be extremely helpful in helping us produce embedded suggestions. "One of the things that's most interesting about *your unconscious* mind is its ability to scan for relevant technical analysis in the charts."

Tag Questions: According to Milton H. Erickson, "Tag Questions displace resistance to the end of a sentence," *don't they?* In addition, they set up a place to create an agreement frame, as well as to strengthen agreement in a pacing situation. It's a fairly effective concept to utilize, *isn't it?* In fact, as we've noticed, all of these language support concepts will greatly enhance your ability to track the reality of the price action and trade successfully, *won't they?*

The More, The More: Once some degree of rapport is established, this construction the incorporation and utilization of otherwise resistant behaviors. "*The more* you try to resist going into a trance, *the more* you find your eyes wanting to shut all by themselves." *The more* you trade, *the more* you find that you must journal your thoughts and log your trades."

Oxymoron means using a combination of words that are a contradiction in terms. For example, "T*ry in vain* to trade without using your journal only to realize that it is vital." Or, "Notice those memories whose joyful pains are as vivid as those whose pleasant sadness can remind you of important lessons from your past trading."

Organ Language is often used in day-to-day language, referring to parts of the body as part of a metaphor, such as, "Trading without stops is a real *pain in the neck*," or "I'm not sure if he's *ready to face* the possibility of trading without rules." "As you develop more and more confidence, it is possible to *reach up to face* many different situations in the price action that would have seemed confusing before." "We are only beginning to *scratch* the surface of this topic. Who *knows* what we might discover about our trading as we journal our thoughts and trades."

Our unconscious mind is not only extremely powerful; it is also obedient—thank goodness! It responds to the pictures that language creates as though the stories and pictures were fact, even if they may not be. The universe is a mathematical construct, meaning that all equations must work in both directions to be valid and to balance. The right side must be balanced and equal to the left. It follows that if we have experienced learned limitations due to the language we have been exposed to and that which we use, there are equal opportunities to experience empowerment from language that is resource based and that the unconscious responds to. In other words, the subconscious language and thoughts act on mental models of the world that are learned limitations and therefore can sabotage our efforts. It can work for us as well by the same process of programming, using language that is vivid, emotionally laden and structurally guided. In the examples above, we can see and grasp that there are myriad ways to communicate effectively with the subconscious. In fact, many of the examples above can be recorded and played by you as you sit in a relaxed state. It is not absolutely necessary to get someone to work with you. Additionally, your voice can be more effective while working with your own unconscious

To reiterate, using "artfully vague" structured language allows a communicator to make statements that sound specific and yet are general enough to be adequately paced for the listener's experience.

Reasons for learning hypnotic language:

- Choose language that is in line with the outcomes we want

- Respect other people's unique interpretations of a situation, especially when we do not know the context

- Recognize when other people are using hypnotic language on us that we can then challenge

- Create space in our language for others (possibly someone we are coaching) to draw on their own resources rather than relying on us for answers

The Power of Metaphor: Language Of The Unconscious Right Brain

"I spent much of my life striving for victory only to realize that real success comes only through surrender!" - Emily Sargent, Councilman

Dual Brain

We have established that your brain has loads to do with your trading. But there are some facts that may help you to support your trading better by understanding the super computer between your ears. The brain has two sides called the right and left hemisphere. They are at first glance identical, but upon closer observation, it becomes apparent that they are not two halves of one brain but two brains in one skull. This is an important distinction to understand and it has vast implications on our thoughts, emotions and behaviors. Schiffe, author of *Two Minds – The Revolutionary Science of Dual Brain Psychology,* wrote:

> "There exists two intact, reasonably intelligent, autonomous minds.
> After these patients had their corpus callosum cut, they each
> manifested two separate minds. They became, two people inhabiting
> one body."

Roger Sperry, psychologist and prominent neuroscientist, performed research that involved "split-brain" patients, people who had had the connection between their left and right brain hemispheres surgically cut as an intervention for epilepsy. His work showed how the two hemispheres function, independently and in concert. He promoted the thought that there are *two* minds. Joseph Bogen, MD, a neurophysiologist on the same Cal Tech research team with Dr. Sperry, thought that this dual-mind concept was very much under-recognized when considering the greatness of Sperry's work. Now, is there any wonder why so much of the market conflict exists in you?

Centuries before Christ, in the 4th century BC, Diocles of Carystus understood that the functions of the two sides of the brain differed. He wrote, "There are two brains in the head, one which gives understanding, and another which provides sense perception." Two ways to approach our environment increases our ability to survive. Having the overall picture serves the animal well for getting around in the world. We quickly have to recognize situations that are safe or that have difficulties, and we need to recognize facial expressions, body movements, frame of mind, and other peoples' or other organisms' intentions toward us. This ability to assess the immediate situation forms the basis of social intelligence and helps judge whether someone is hostile or friendly. At same time, rapid and precise actions need simplicity of attention and, of course, chart-analysis is no different. Being able to assess the reflection of the electronic terrain of the charts requires both intuition and precision. A human animal can't spend its life forever searching the data stream horizon. A response (trade decision) needs to be made, and it has to be on continuous, coordinated movement—even when staying in a cash position. The individual needs to make a sequence of precise, rapid-fire decisions, and this decision-making seems best done by the left-brain. Similarly, in speech, one particular word has to follow the one before; we can't say everything at once. For this, an ordered sequencer is most useful.

In humans, sequential ability underlies logic and language. Let's take the monkey as an example—since they are rumored to be our distant relatives—to illustrate how sequential ability is manifest. Anthropologist Gordon Gallup describes a kind of grammar necessary to swing through the trees. So, what's important to recognize is that the animal that remembered better these sequential or "grammatical" movements would survive to produce more offspring. The trader that establishes a sequential routine based upon effective behavioral protocols will survive to trade successfully.

Cognition. Language sets the definition of what we view as reality. When we have no word for something we tend to not be aware of the concept. Learning to read and write in youth influences the development of the hemispheres and the way they work. Benjamin Lee Whorf, author of *Language, Thought & Reality,* uses the example of the word 'snow'. the Eskimos have so many words for it because they see it in so many different forms.

Emotions. Richard Davidson, PhD, Vilas Professor of Psychology and Psychiatry at Harvard, in a series of studies showed that the left hemisphere might involve different emotions than the right. The conventional wisdom of the past indicated that the right was playful and happy, with spontaneity. But, based on more recent studies, the left hemisphere seems to involve positive emotions like happiness and the right, negative emotions like anger. Working with newborns he found the same kind of brain patterns with significant activation of the left, in happy moods, the right in fear, anger and disgust. This means that the difference in the hemispheric emotions, measured by their asymmetries in brain electrical activity, exist at birth. Why is negativity on right side? It may have to do with the issue of control and the safety that knowing and awareness brings. Organization and sequential logic can be very comforting and lead to optimism, whereas the intangible, the unclear, the ambiguous can be troubling and fearful. Can you think of a better definition of the markets than intangible, unclear in predictive quality, and ambiguous in character? It will move as it will, so we have even more reason to be troubled and fearful at first pass when taking risk in the markets. However, armed with this information about emotion and the left and right brains, we can then develop ways to impact upon the way our unconscious negative emotions can be given expression. Awareness and using exercises that help the right brain to both purge, express and process difficult emotions will go a long way to controlling disruptive urges that can suck your capital right out of your trading account.

Perception. The ability to see the big picture involves both hemispheres and the nature of perception is impacted upon by the orientation of the dominant or left hemisphere. How is perception determined by hemisphere dominance for Right and for Left? The good news is that the right brain has an innate ability to tolerate ambiguity; however, the bad news is that there is a tendency to fear, morbidity, and negativism. But the right brain is much more flexible and prone to explore "different" ways to approach items (creative). What does this mean for your trading? Well, develop intuitive analysis and train your right brain to "see" the charts from various angles and learn to listen to your gut. This is much different from winging it impulsively, which is what leads to "issues." The left may be more rigid, but it is usually happier; however, it may not tolerate ambiguity well. So, we can begin to see that who shows up to trade is determined also by what brain you're firing from.

Behavior. There is almost nothing that is regulated solely by the left or right hemisphere. Both get involved as soon as any situation becomes slightly more complex. And both are at work all the time. That is why there are times when conflict is raging inside. Consider these anecdotes from the archives of split-brain surgeries performed to positively impact upon epilepsy. When this surgery is performed, the individual by most accounts seems normal, but when we look a little closer we find:

- The man who tried to hit his wife with his right hand while his left tried to stop him.

- The man who tried to light a cigarette with his left hand while his right tried to pull it out.

- The woman who went to take a dress from her closet with her right hand while her left would put it back.

- The woman who abruptly woke because she was slapped only to realize that she had slapped herself. The right had awakened and heard the alarm, while the left was still sleep and attempted to wake her because she was late.

The dual brain has two distinct brain systems in which one analyzes piece-by-piece, detailing changes and the other makes an overall update and applies it until the next change. This dual function might well have offered a greater advantage:

1) That there would be redundancy in checking conclusions about the nature of events and plans for possible action.

2) Two very specialized ways to deal with the world.

A snapshot of left and right brain functions.

Brain development is like city development. Often, early growth was without a plan; it developed as result of water, or a spur from a train, etc.

List of conventional wisdom's hemispheric attributes:

LEFT (Analytic)	RIGHT (Global)
Successive Hemispheric Style	Simultaneous Hemispheric Style
1. Verbal	1. Visual, tactual, kinesthetic
2. Responds to word meaning	2. Responds to word pitch, feeling
3. Sequential	3. Random
4. Processes information linearly	4. Processes information in chunks
5. Responds to logic	5. Responds to emotion
6. Plans ahead	6. Spontaneous
7. Recalls people's names	7. Recalls people's faces
8. Speaks with few gestures	8. Gestures when speaking
9. Punctual	9. Less punctual
10. Prefers formal study design	10. Prefers sound/music background
11. Prefers bright lights while studying	11. Prefers frequent mobility while studying

Now that we have taken a look at some of the functions of the left and right brain and the general importance of each to your trading success, let's take a look at one of the right brain's most powerful tools for healing and change—metaphor.

Metaphor is the language of the right brain and it permeates our lives. To get something done we "step up to the plate." With difficult choices, we're "doing heavy lifting." We "grab the bull by the horns" to "break the ice." The lexicon is replete with metaphor, and it is powerful. Metaphor can be riveting, motivating, captivating, enticing, mesmerizing, elegant, simple, elaborate, and highly effective. Emotions are activated on unconscious levels through metaphor due to the rich symbolic association with concepts, both painful and pleasurable, in our subconscious. Metaphors tie into the images of our unconscious and solicit hopes, fears, and longings.

Carl Jung spoke of the strength of the archetype. In Jung's psychological framework, archetypes are innate, universal prototypes for ideas and may be used to interpret observations. A group of memories and interpretations associated with an archetype are a complex, e.g. a *mother complex* associated with the *mother archetype*. Jung treated the archetypes as psychological organs, analogous to physical ones in that both are morphological givens that arose through evolution. Milton Erickson, the grandfather of clinical hypnosis in the US, used metaphor and stories to speak directly to his patients' subconscious and initiate unconscious resources to bear on issues that presented obstacles to them. His storytelling manner both relaxed and put at ease patients' conscious minds as he began to engage them on an unconscious level.

Metaphors can be life affirming or a denying metaphor that would present as a mental/psychic structure that embodies the individual's rules for living, and for our purposes, her rules of trading, as in "the market's out to get me." Also, to create substantive change, it's important to identify and reframe/restructure/redefine and alter the underlying metaphors that drive our stories about what's going on in the price action. As discussed in earlier chapters, we have in our MAPs, paradigms and mental models symbols that embody rich and complex structures of metaphor. For example, when we think of things like love, war, birth, death, success, marriage or money, the dynamic is multi-varied with associations and cross associations relating both directly and indirectly to our sense of self, relationship to others, familial bonds, fears of success, and fears of failure. And, through the global interconnectedness of the markets, when we participate, we are putting and pitting all of the psychological and cultural variables that impact upon our psyche as a "trading persona" against it. Furthermore, as we move and shift our paradigms surrounding these underlying metaphors that are not working for us, it is important to identify and then transfer the cultural/organizational/personal lessons, and this happens most steadfastly through metaphor modifications. For example, "I am a loser if I don't make money on this trade." Metaphors establish the door to creativity as in pictures, sounds, physical feelings, tastes and smells, which can be woven together or individually focused as metaphor or symbols that define who we are and what we do.

Right-brain mediated exercises help with strengthening intuition, development of right brain analysis and communication between the two brain/minds. Some of these exercises are:

- Role play

- Letter writing

- Dance

- Poetry

- Ritual

- Trance

- Hypnosis

- Guided imagery

Change comes from facing fears, and doing things differently. Using old and ineffective strategies to address new challenges is like using your old boxcar to go on the freeway. Identify a state—like the state of intense focus, or the state of relaxed detachment but fully present, or the state of curious fun as in doing a crossword or playing chess—one that is new or novel and like that of having taken a test when you received a very high grade. You embodied a relaxed focus and you were tuned into the flow of the questions in such a way that it was pleasurable but aligned. Begin to research and study trading patterns in this state. Develop a routine with a set of steps that does not waiver. Ensure that this state is nurtured and used for "every" period of study and paper trading by shifting gears consciously for each trade simulation and actual trade. Repeat until it seems out-of-the-ordinary not to do it. Old habits and patterns must not only be interrupted but also replaced with new patterns that have been reinforced through repetition. This process will be explained in greater detail in a later chapter.

Meta-Messages

It is often said that the price action discounts all known news. In other words, all that is known about an equity, future, currency, option, or other financial instrument is priced into whatever bid/ask level that instrument is currently trading at. Remember the market is a reflection of all the decision points, hopes, fears and greed of human beings that could otherwise be called organic variables. This means that the market is virtually organic as well; it moves, undulates, pulsates, and surges with the masses. At any moment, it contains all the conceivable knowns that humans resonate with. As humans, our systems are subject to the same "meta" relationship. Meta refers in this instance to the Greek derivation of "beyond." What we do is based on what we think and what we think is directly related to our MAPS, mental models and paradigms that have been discussed. When we communicate, we are also communicating an idea.

We are not only talking but also using our bodies, including eye movement, posture, muscle movement, voice pitch, tone, timbre and force. In any given moment, we are communicating in a meta-way, meaning that there is a great amount of information sent unconsciously, and received both unconsciously for a portion of the communication and consciously for other portions.

So, a meta-message is what's communicated but not said. The meaning of the communication is the effect that it has. If you are attempting to blame someone else, or even worse, blaming the market for decisions that you have made, you are abdicating your responsibility and you are also communicating a message about yourself (that of inflexibility, constriction of thought and lack of ability to see reality) that will be lost to you because it is beyond your awareness. And, the beauty of the market is that, try as we may—and we do try very hard—it is virtually impossible to place the onus of our actions in the market participation on someone or something else. To be healthily engaged in meta-messages is to be in a continuous learning position. What was I thinking? Where did that behavior of mine come from? What was I looking at when I placed this trade?

Part of the meta-message is the metaphor. Metaphor is an extremely powerful aspect of our humanness. Everything in the metaphor carries information about the whole. It holds reams of stories in one symbol, image, behavior, and/or saying. "A picture is worth a thousand words" is a well-known and broadly shared euphemism. By the same token, all environments tell a story. Our surroundings are an expression of decisions we make, compromises we have agreed to, goals we have achieved, desires and obligations. What does your trading environment say about you? How you dress, talk, eat, interact with others, meet other's needs, and demonstrate skill levels, to name a few, all impact upon the metaphors of your life. Additionally, your beliefs are integrally melded in as well, and affect deeply the tapestry of your game.

Use these factors to uncover your hidden stories about your beliefs and your conscious and unconscious metaphors. Aligning behavior with desired outcomes is intertwined in a meta-message. But first it's important to bring to awareness and learn about your hidden stories and beliefs. The goal is to empower yourself and reflect the inner intentions about being successful in the market—to make the outer a reflection of the inner. This is not only the most powerful form of influence for your unconscious, but it is also a way of teaching yourself through awareness and congruency. Take for instance the man who works in a dark and cluttered office. When the price action goes against him, he yells, screams, and swears. If his day is down it is reflected in poor and maligned treatment of those around him. He blames the noise, the weather, the computer, the news, and anyone and anything else for his shortcomings, and he wonders why he can't seem to profit.

Strategies for Successful Living and Trading

Sometimes I lie awake at night, and I ask, "Where have I gone wrong?"
Then a voice says to me, "This is going to take more than one night." -
Charles Schultz, Charlie Brown in *Peanuts*

We are creatures of habit. Our choices follow patterns we take with us wherever we go. It is our patterns in thinking and behaving that create our response to our circumstances, not the circumstances themselves. Only by becoming aware of these patterns or habits can we begin to choose the life we want. Running away from what we don't want is a strategy for ineffective results. It is much more goal oriented and proactive to be deliberate and intentional about moving toward what we do want. Circumstances are products of either our choices or the environment, so we are creating future circumstances all the time. Unless we choose to look within to uncover and review those patterns that are making our lives what they are, we will continually follow the same patterns we have set regardless of how much we say we want to change.

Strategies for Success

Patterns of habits are not strategies, at least not in the vein of goal orientation. A strategy is a sequence of thoughts and behaviors that follow from a set of beliefs and a sense of self. We have learned strategies that can work for us or against us, once we are aware of what we are doing.

Every move, every gesture, every natural speech sample, reveals the patterns of our strategies and the way we run our lives as a whole. If we pay attention to those gestures and speech patterns, we will learn and become aware of our improvable and, in that way, we will be able to coach ourselves.

In my grandfather's old collection of LP albums, some of those albums have been scratched in ways that create grooves within grooves. Our patterns are like grooves, our behavior defaults to those pattern groups. Once the grooves are cut, the easiest choice is to do what we have done before, to follow that groove, doing the same ineffective things we've done before. Even if it has worked in the past, it may still need to be revamped, especially when dealing with strategies for trading. The markets change and part of that change is cyclical, and part of it may be based on entirely new circumstances, demographics or otherwise, to which the markets are reacting . If we cannot or will not remain open to strategy/pattern modification, we will find ourselves on the losing end of the order flow. Of course, this has to do with our pre-market participatory behavior as well, which can set us up for distortion and compulsion. You may be familiar with the expression, "If it ain't broke, don't fix it." Today it is more likely that if it ain't broke, it is probably redundant. Each moment holds another opportunity, and when that moment has lapsed, so has the opportunity; there are no second chances or "do-overs" for that moment.

Successful strategies begin with an affirmative intention about as many aspects or points of view of the impending event or trade(s) as possible. Being deliberate, focused, and open with curiosity and flexibility about the trading environment is part and parcel to a successful trading strategy.

Coding Strategies

When I was in college, I knew a guy, Kyle, who was a great basketball player. He did not begin as a great b-baller. In fact he did not play much his freshman year. But everyday he would watch the older, more accomplished players. He studied the way they moved, the way they practiced, the way the held the ball, the way they dribbled and played defense, the way they hustled, and the way they talked with passion. He studied how they stretched and how hard they worked out. He saw himself going through practice as if it were a game. Moving as they moved. With every play that he learned, he imagined himself going through all of the steps. By feeling the leather of the ball, hearing the swish of the nets, feeling how his body felt when he dribbled through the defense for a lay-up or charged the basket for a rebound, seeing the wholeness of the court and sensing a balance of where everyone was, he would feel the passion for playing, the excitement of each step. By coding this strategy, he became a great player.

The Above and Below Are Strategies

John is a trader. He wants to play the Friday morning, 8:30 AM EDT NonFarm Payroll Economic Report. He lives on the west coast, so it comes at 5:30 AM his time. He stays up with his buddies the night before, drinking, and gets home a little late—something that he does often. When the alarm rings, he snoozes just a little more, but awakens with enough time to dash to his computer and pull up his platform. He has tried to get up early enough in the past to practice yoga and stretch, and then have a little breakfast before taking a look at the world markets, but it has been difficult to maintain, especially when he has a slight hangover. He's already a little anxious because his portfolio has taken several drawdowns lately, and he is thinking that he "needs" to get back some of those losses. He decides to increase his contract size on the Futures Index he's playing so that he can "get his money back." At the appointed time he looks over at the report, but the numbers are not in yet. He decides that the numbers are going to be positive and places an order to buy 5 contracts where he normally plays 2 due to his portfolio size. He doesn't place a stop, thinking that he will keep one in his head. Suddenly the tick shoots way up and he is elated. It goes up and up and his P/L is correspondingly high, John starts to do the money dance. Then, without warning about 2 minutes into the 5-minute chart that he is playing off, the tick begins to retrace and falls precipitously down, and down more and down more into negative territory. It then picks up steam and drops like a red brick. He panics, and when it has fallen over 3 points against him he doubles down hoping that it will come back. It falls another 5 points before the next 2 bars close. Now he is 8 points and several thousand dollars down as the tick then stalls and moves sideways.

Strategies are more than patterns of thinking. They consist of the way we structure our beliefs, our values, our sense of purpose, our sense of identity, how we process information, how we behave and more. However, if we start with a simple approach to modeling, it may make more sense. The following is an example of the basic internal and external stimulus coding elements:

- Ve - Visual external—an image that we see externally

- Vir - Visual internal remembered—an image in our mind that we remember

- Vic - Visual internal construct—an image that we create in our minds

- Air - Auditory internal remembered—a sound we remember

- Aic - Auditory internal construct—a sound that we construct

- Ke - Kinesthetic external—a feeling that we experience physically

- Ki - Kinaesthetic internal—emotion we feel

Coding Your Trading

Example of the above:

- Visual/external (Ve) = A trading log with money management calculations, a trading journal with your name at the top, a check made out to your favorite charity. You "see" the trading log and journal and check as separate visualizations, seeing them clearly and in detail; something you'd like to see as part of being a successful trader.

- Visual/Internal/remembered (Vir) = A trade/investment that was a winner, your portfolio increase. This is a vision of a memory of an actual event. You see it clearly and in detail, notice the colors, whether it's night or day, inside or out, the computer screen and the way it portrays your information.

- Visual/internal/construct (Vic) = Seeing self go through a morning routine as a pre-market participation exercise, cashing a million-dollar broker check. Detailed construction of a behavior you want to incorporate as a habit and new pattern.

- A sound we remember auditory/internal/remembered (Air) = "you're awesome – internal voice," a compliment from a colleague on a winning trade. As you remember the circumstances of the auditory memory, notice the tone and pitch of the voice.

- A sound that we construct (Aic) = Hearing the voice of someone commenting that they appreciate the adroit money management and skillful analysis you employ to make winning trades; an inner dialogue. Saying to self , "That was a good job."

- A feeling we experience physically (Ke) = the feel of the keyboard or mouse when inputting information for an order and then a stop loss.

- An emotion we feel (Ki) = the desire to plan your trade and the passion to trade your plan; having a sense of satisfaction and empowerment from keeping your personal commitments.

Revisiting John's Example Above

He stays up the night before drinking, gets up later than he had committed to, and dashes to the computer (Ke - Kinesthetic external). He then pulls up his platform

(Ke – Kinesthetic external) and (Ve – Visual external). He has tried to get up early enough in the past to practice yoga and stretch, and then have a little breakfast before taking a look at the world markets, but he has told himself it's too difficult to maintain (Aic – Auditory internal construct), especially when he has a slight hangover and berates himself (Aic – Auditory internal construct). He's already a little anxious (Ki – Kinesthetic internal) because his portfolio has taken several drawdowns lately, and he has told himself before he needs to get back some of his losses (Air – Auditory internal remembered). He decides (tells himself) to increase his contract size so he can "get his money back" (Aic – Auditory internal construct). He looks over at the report (Ve – Visual External), but the numbers are not in yet. He thinks or tells himself the numbers are going to be positive (Aic – Auditory internal construct) and places an order to buy 5 contracts (Ke – Kinesthetic external) where he normally plays 2 (Ve – Visual internal remembered). He doesn't place a stop, thinking he will keep one in his head (Aic – Auditory internal construct). Suddenly the tick shoots way up and he is elated (Ki – Kinesthetic internal). John starts to do the money dance (Ke – Kinesthetic external). The tick begins to retrace and falls precipitously down into negative territory. He panics (Ki – Kinesthetic internal). He doubles down (Ke – Kinesthetic external) hoping (Ki – Kinesthetic internal) it will come back. It doesn't...

The code for a losing strategy:

Ke -> Ke -> Ve -> Aic -> Aic ->Ki -> Air -> Aic -> Ve ->

Aic -> Ke -> Ve -> Aic -> Ki -> Ke -> Ki -> Ke -> Ki

Once you have mastered each point in the code examples, you are ready to use them to identify the skills you want to code using all of the visual, auditory, and kinesthetic (physical and emotional) elements that go into that skill set. You'll want to track the sequential series of experiences connected with each of those elements. For example, before trading, before the actual market participation, during the trade, and upon exiting. This strategy is like playing chess with a beginning, middle and end game, only with trading you have the preparation, the participation, which includes the entry and lastly, the exit. Another way to say it would be "the beginning" or "approach" to the market (what you see, think, feel and do)—getting in (what you see, think, feel and do) then the exit (what you see, think, feel and do). This may sound quite elementary and redundant; however, if you are struggling, that means your strategy is ineffective and the only way to transform a losing strategy into a winning strategy is to break it down into its primary components. You've got to break the code and reassemble it, modify it, and change it so it becomes a winning strategy. You can't change what you can't face and you can't face what you don't know. To model a skill, we have to want to do it and believe we can do it.

Why it is Important to Learn How to Model

"I do not feel obliged to believe that the same God who has endowed us with sense, reason, and intellect has intended us to forgo their use." - Galileo Galilei

As children, we learn to model by observing our environment and using all of our senses to gather information. From this observation, we begin to develop strategies to get the results we want and, in many cases, these strategies are developed intuitively. But the higher and more complicated our objectives, the more important it is that our strategies be conscious in order to optimize the structure. And to do this, we must consistently look for and be receptive to feedback from our environment to:

a) Determine what strategies we are employing to get a result

b) b) Modify or change that strategy if we're not getting the results we hoped for

One of the ways to increase your chances of modeling success is to use a template to lay your modeling structure upon. One-way to do that is the Test Operate Test Exit method or TOTE.

The principal underlying TOTE is that our behavior is driven or motivated by an outcome. We recognize when we have achieved the outcome by a unique set of evidence criteria (i.e., what we will be seeing, hearing, and feeling when we have achieved the outcome, the vision of success). We are constantly comparing our present state or reality to our desired state or future reality to find out if they match. When they do match, we know we have reached the exit and have achieved our outcome. If the present state does not match the desired state, we must complete another operation to discover if that makes a difference.

We are running TOTEs throughout our lives comparing where we are with where we want to be, taking actions to bring us closer, and eventually to, the exit itself. Examples of this in everyday life include:

- Learning to walk - we try and fail, changing this and that until we are successful

- Riding a bike

- Learning to play a game

- Learning a subject in school

Another example from modeling business leaders is that these leaders keep going until they have reached a successful exit, whatever it takes, whereas others—those who do not naturally excel as leaders—exit before the original desired outcome. This may be due to fatigue, time decay, distraction, distortion, or loss of confidence in their own ability to achieve the outcome.

When Kyle, the basketball player, became successful from modeling his winning team members' strategies, he was running a TOTE. He tried, failed, modified, tried, failed, modified, tried, and so forth. You get the picture. He tested, operated and checked for a match in desired outcome (state) vs. outcome (state) attained. If the outcomes or states are not equal and do not match, then back to operation #2, test again. If no match, then operation #3, then test and so on until they MATCH, then exit.

When Kyle's basketball outcomes, i.e., dribbling, passing, defense, and shooting, all matched the desired outcome, he exited the TOTE for that time, only to be repeated when he identified another level of outcome of state to achieve. At that point, he would again run the TOTE until he achieved the match. Furthermore, TOTEs can exist within TOTEs. For example, dribbling can be a TOTE, passing can be a TOTE, and so forth. Some TOTEs run every few minutes, some every few hours, days, weeks or years. Another word in our lexicon for TOTEs is practice; however, it is important to understand the concept of TOTEs because the level of specificity greatly supports the system alignment and effective coding of the successful strategy. To just say "practice" is to leave much of the process incomplete. Essentially, the TOTE is a feedback loop designed to prompt you to find what you need to achieve your desired state. Key skills for successfully navigating the TOTE in order to be able to model are: sensitivity to what is happening, a willingness to learn from feedback, and the flexibility to do or learn something different when what you are doing is not working.

John would help himself tremendously if he:

a) Formulated a vision for the state or desired outcome

b) Determined what details were necessary to achieve that state by modeling someone who is successful

c) Determined or decoded his strategy to short circuit or interrupt ineffective patterns so that they do not compromise any new strategies

d) Developed and began to run TOTEs in order to get closer to a desired state of outcomes that match with current state of outcomes

Professional traders have TOTEs; they are called successful trades. When we follow our rules, we are initiating a TOTE to take us to a successful exit, part of which looks like pulling the trigger at just the right time with successful entries and exits. But often, without rigorous examination of our patterns, it is difficult to determine why our current outcome states do not match our desired outcome states. Only through critical thinking, examination and questioning can we find out which operations in the TOTE are missing. When that happens, these should prompt an immediate modification of the pattern; either through testing operations or through modeling someone who does it better.

If you are modeling an individual, the key is not just to ask the person that you are modeling to tell you what they do, because what they think they know and what they really know about what they do are two very different things. It is key to either watch them trade intently, or, if that is not possible, to have the subject imagine that they are trading in order for them to identify their nuance operations. By modeling, we discover the structure by which we, and others, are getting results. By choosing the important qualities that lead to desired state outcomes, we get the results we value. We are then, in turn, able to model this behavior as we have incorporated the successful strategy and can form the pattern or habit of repeating the successful strategy while remaining flexible enough to continually look for feedback in our environment, so that, when necessary, our strategy can be modified again for improvement.

Tools and Techniques for High-Performance Trading

"The best hope for the human race is if enough individuals do their inner work." - C.G. Jung

Modeling Excellence

Modeling is an extremely proficient strategy for pursuing success in any performance-oriented endeavor. As the saying goes, "If someone can do it, anyone can do it." Let's look more closely at what modeling is:

- Modeling is a state of curiosity and selflessness. It is a desire to listen to, watch, respect, and learn from others as well as ourselves.

- Modeling is an interest in process over content. Process or the "how" something is done is arguably more important than content or the "what." The process is where skill is focused to create the end result. There are countless ways to do anything, but there are ways that are extremely effective and there are time-and-energy wasters that might get you to the same result eventually, only to be scathed by the inherent procedural shortcomings.

- Modeling can take many forms. Some of your most fundamental skills will have been acquired through modeling others. Babies and young children are expert modelers. Only when they start learning by more traditional methods do they begin to lose this skill.

- Once you've identified the mastery in an individual who does well the thing you wish to capture, you can model anything. For example:

    o   Motivation of self

    o   Influence

    o   Achieving a personal best

- o Listening

- o Networking

Equally, you can develop an excellent ability to: Get depressed

- Sulk

- Worry

- Resist change

- Respond compulsively

- React impulsively

- Freeze in the face of fear

With conscious awareness, you have a choice to do something different.

Mentoring. Finding and "sitting next to an expert" is an excellent way to model skillful behavior. The subject being modeled can also benefit from this process by learning, from feedback, how they structure their experience. Just because someone does something well, that doesn't mean they necessarily know how they are able to capture successful results. With this awareness the "unconscious competent" can achieve greater consistency in the skills they have.

Applying the process to self, we can see that the strategy is to reproduce an ability or skill you possess in another area of life, in order to use it in other contexts. For instance, you may be methodical, self-assured and cautious in another part of your life, but highly anxious, impulsive and unpredictable when it comes to trading. This is a common occurrence. Talk to traders who will be happy to tell you how their rules "went out the window" as soon as they felt the pain of a position going against them and they found they moved their stop, or double-downed, or violated their rules in some other way. Or, they were paralyzed by panic when the tick went against them and impulsively exited what looked like a losing trade, only to see the price action move in their favor just a few bars later, turning what appeared to be a loser into a winner.

Uncovering these strategies involves observing personal program(s) that are sequences of mental and behavioral codes. For instance, how we do what we do when we walk, talk, drive, read, or laugh? Normally we don't think of how we do these things, but they constitute a code of established behavior. The programs that make them happen are managed on your behalf by your unconscious mind. These are known as strategies. When you have the strategy for how someone manages his or her experience, you have the key to reproducing that experience for yourself.

"When a chef produces a gourmet dinner, not only is he following a recipe for the ingredients, he is also following a recipe for thinking and behavior. He may have an image of what he wants the dish to look like accompanied by the aroma of the final meal. He may also be concerned with timing and the look and feel of the ingredients. He has a unique way of achieving the result." - Jane Knight, *NLP at Work*

Trading has context specific patterns that produce excellence around things like:

- Effective planning

- Rules setting

- Position sizing

- Money management

- Technical analysis

- Fundamental analysis

But these are not all. There are ancillary aims, concepts and frames-of-mind that indirectly supports your success. Often you will hear really successful traders share that they have a consistent pattern for selflessness—a notion of giving back, which reminds them they are a part of a larger community. They report that this perspective helps them to maintain a grounded perspective of in the face of greed. Secondly, they have a larger reason why they desire to be successful, one not money driven. They have a skill in using metaphor and visionary thinking. Winning traders are able to create a sensory rich vision of success that creates a subconscious passion for remaining focused on what matters most; keeping rules and following their plan. They also have a dedication to sequential and purpose-driven protocols, i.e., the development of strong habits and a routine based in proven methods of success. These are additional strong concepts incorporated in many highly skilled and successful traders.

A strategy is a global, overarching plan designed to achieve a specific result; for instance "winning." Once a strategy has been identified, it can be refined by breaking into segments the specific thoughts and behaviors that produce the desired results. For instance, when playing chess, there is an open where the pieces are moved to initiate a strategy. After the open, the strategy is envisioned several moves ahead, taking into account what you will do if your opponent responds in various ways. Then, the pieces are moved accordingly. At certain junctures, you stop and possibly stand up or walk around the board to gain a "new" perspective. In other words, you think, and then do, shifting between certain body movements to optimize your thinking, and then you move again. In this modeling process, you are looking at all of the "pieces" of thinking and behavior that produce the outcome.

With modeling a trading strategy, there is the same attention to detail in how you do what you do. Similarly, if you were to model the routines of a successful trader, you would break down both their thinking and doing process, getting a template of how they do what they do. Actually, there is a joy in modeling, especially as you consider the one being modeled is actually highly proficient in trading in the way you would like to trade. You can refine the model by testing which elements add to excellence and which detract or make no difference. By taking one element at a time, you can determine how this affects the overall result. This enables you to generate the most effective model, which you can use to teach others.

Modeling enables you to uncover natural skill, the uniqueness of self, the quality of inborn talent and developed skill in things like chart reading, indicator usage, pattern discovery, technical analysis aptitude, fundamental analysis grasp, and trading strategy formation adeptness. Modeling identification and model-following help to consistently raise the bar from competence to excellence. Whether you are a "lone wolf" trader or part of a mastermind group, you are still part of a larger system, a community, a family of like-minded individuals. As a conscious member of the larger community, you support yourself by supporting the efforts of others. As you pay attention to the role you play in the larger system, you add to your own trading health by reaching out and sharing your thoughts and viewpoints. As others thrive, so too do you, when you have a purpose to contribute to this bigger system in a positive way—that is, to add value. It's important to also maintain both an ethical and ecological mindset as you approach your trading as a part of a whole. Principle Centered Trading, both the principles of human interaction and self-growth, as well as the principles of sound monetary dynamics, are empowering to your trading well-being.

There are important questions to ask while in the modeling process. For instance:

What are your myths, beliefs and unconscious stories around money and the abundance or lack of it?

What are your beliefs about losing money, failure, trading troughs and drawdowns?

What are your beliefs about learning and its relationship to trading?

Also, it is of great importance to be aware of your beliefs surrounding the following:

- *Your mental ability.* For example, if you believe you are mentally inferior or simply not a smart person, this will infect your ability to perform by creating distortions and a self-fulfilling prophesy of less-than emotions. It's not a question of whether it's actually true. If you believe under the surface, far out of your awareness, that you aren't smart enough, then you won't be.

- *Your worthiness.* Some people, on subliminal levels, don't believe they deserve to win, even though outwardly they muster the fortitude to put forth the effort. But when the rubber-meets-the-road, their tires invariably blow out, careening them off the path and into oncoming traffic. You will find a way to "create" in reality what you believe deeply. That is why it is so important to increase your awareness of what myths you are holding close to your chest.

- *Ability to tolerate risk.* We are all risk takers. We are at risk every day to things like pathogens in the air, accidents, traffic and travel. Most people don't perceive it in this context, but whenever we walk out of our doors, we take on a level of environmental risk. It is important to know what your current level of tolerance is and what your current internal stories about risk are. I'm not suggesting you will or want to be a daredevil with your denars or drachmas; however, putting courage into context around winning and what is necessary for you to embrace it will require some, if not lots, of tolerance for risk. And, viewing it in the frame that best serves your goals will be supportive to reaching them. But you can't modify something you have no awareness of.

- *Knowledge or lack of it.* You will want to find out what you don't know. I may not have had much affinity for our former Defense Secretary, Donald Rumsfeld, but he took a beating and was made fun of for talking about known unknowns and unknown unknowns. However, it is true that, if you are not aware of the level of your ignorance, and you don't know what you don't know, you can unnecessarily spend a lot of cash by either laboring in ignorance and making many, many mistakes, or by enrolling in classes that will be more than happy to teach you things about trading—things you don't need. It's like trying to maneuver in a dark space you've never been in; if you don't know what obstacles are around you, then negotiating movement can be quite difficult; and in the wrong space, like walking across a high precipice in the dark, you could lose your life. Because somebody turns on a light, that doesn't mean all your challenges are over. It just means the unknowns (how you're going to traverse it) are now within your awareness. All you've got to do is figure out a strategy for the unknown that seemed nearly impossible just before the light was focused onto the path.

- *Ability to ask for help.* For the aficionados of risqué humor, there is an obscure character named "Dolemite" in a story of the same name, by Rudy Ray Morre, an actor, producer and writer. Dolemite was heard to tell an unsuspecting neophyte who was trying to do something shady: "You come into the world with your nose all snotty. If you don't know the game, you'd better ask somebody." Men are usually guiltier of this than women, like refusing to ask for directions when lost (guys and gals, you know who you are). The point is that, if you believe you don't need help and you don't need to ask credible sources about issues you may have, then what you are asking is for the market to take your money, which it does gladly. I remember Sydney, a good acquaintance who almost lost his nest egg and house because he was unwilling to get help with his trading. He told me that he had to "do it himself." He finally learned some skill sets from his mistakes; however, the cost of his experience almost took all that he had.

- *Whether you have or will ever have enough of "what it takes."* What are your beliefs about what it will take to achieve your goals? Too many traders and investors think the markets are a get-rich-quick game. These are usually individuals who are quite new. Even some of you who have been in the markets for a year or so may harbor myths about what is possible and how fast it can happen. The pros will tell you trading is not easy or quick. If fact, the more you hold on to this fable, the faster you will part ways with your hard earned cash. I'm not talking about betting the farm or playing the trading lotto game. You might get lucky...once or twice. But, if you plan on trading for any length of time, you would be well advised to embrace it as though trading were like traveling around the world on foot: it takes 1 step at a time, while being methodical, focused, cautious and fully aware of your surroundings. As the saying goes, "If you want to survive, pay attention!"

- *Change and the tolerance for ambiguity or the lack thereof.* The markets are full of ambiguity. What are your beliefs about being right? Is that one of your issues? If it is, you'd better root it out quickly. You may use all the indicators you can fit into a chart; you can back-test to your hearts content; you can identify all the patterns that you like; and still the market will do what it's going to do. You may increase the "probability" of correctly identifying the direction the market will take, but you will never, ever be able to fully predict *with certainty* that the market will do something at a particular juncture. You must be willing to lose, for the market is a game of percentages and probability. If you can't tolerate the ambiguity and be willing to lose, then you may want to identify something else into which to put your money and your precious time.

- *Your capacity for emotional tolerance.* Do you have any idea about your emotional trigger points? What are your beliefs about your emotional intelligence? In his book, *Emotional Intelligence*, Daniel Goleman discusses the importance of awareness and personal management. I would add to that personal leadership. What I mean by personal leadership is taking stock of your improvables and making a list of your personal expectancies and how you aim to achieve them; then monitoring your progress using a scorecard. One thing is for sure-- if you can't master, or at least come to grips with, out-of-control emotions, then you'd do better to give your money to a program trader.

- *Your capacity for consistency.* What are your underlying beliefs about remaining consistent and the importance to trading? I've commented at length about the importance of establishing protocols, routines, and habits. Find out if you have contravening concepts in your subconscious about your ability to do what it takes consistently.

Understand your capabilities. In the words of Clint Eastwood's character, Dirty Harry, "A man's gotta know his limitations." In other words, be aware of your capacity for or your openness to things like:

- Flexibility

- Goal-oriented behavior

- Sensitivity and intuitiveness

- Learning

- Walking the talk around protocols

- Change

- Availability to the critical importance of feedback

Monitor yourself and become aware of your behavior by:

- Asking for feedback

- Changing to increase flexibility while remaining true to values

- Acting and speaking from mission/vision/and self-interested beliefs

- Taking responsibility for all trading decisions

The following is a process for modeling a skill:

1. Identify the skills you want to model and reproduce. Be specific. For example, you may want to:

a. Use indicators with greater ease and efficiency

b. Use macro and microwave knowledge to capture more market gain

c. Make better entry and exit decisions

d. Start the day with a strong and positive frame of mind

2. Select a person (or people) who demonstrates excellence in the skill. Choose the top performer. Be sure you understand you *learn* excellence by *replicating* excellence. Define excellence in terms of the results you want to achieve. Choose a model that exemplifies the results, and also ensure the achievement of those results resonates with how you want to trade. It will do you little good to model a very successful day trading scalper who makes money by trading many times during the day when you have little patience for that and prefer longer time-frames in which to trade. Once you have the model or mentor you want to emulate, you will define excellence in terms of what she sees, hears, feels and does when she is displaying her skill.

3. You will want observe your model in action to identify the following:

a. What specifically they do and how do they do it

b. Any subtle behavior patterns—their eye movements and their nonverbal behavior

c. How they manage their environment

    i. Computer placement, monitors, indicators, news feeds, reports, macro and micro economics

d. Their language patterns—which filter(s) they use

e. What beliefs and values they demonstrate and express

      f.   How they communicate a sense of identity

      g.   What purpose they seem to fulfill, or say they fulfill

4. Question your model. First, ensure they associate into an experience when using the skill you wish to model—in other words, they are in touch with their physical, mental and emotional body so they can accurately describe how they do what they do. When you are certain they are associated (imagining themselves using the skill), be sure to phrase your questions in the present tense to keep them associated, e.g., "What are you seeing?" "What are you saying to yourself," and so on. You are interested in the "what" and the "how" of what they do and not the "why." Check out their thinking at each of the logical levels. For example, you can ask them:

      a.   What are you aware of in your environment?

      b.   What are you saying and doing? (It's useful to compare this with what they actually said and did in your observations.)

      c.   What are you thinking? (watch their eye movements, which will give more information about their internal strategy than their conscious answer to the question). If you notice them using visual eye accessing cues, for example, ask them, "What do you see?"

      d.   What are your capabilities? One of them will be the skill you are modeling.

      e.   What is important to you at this time? (this is to elicit values.)

      f.   What do you believe?" About yourself, about others, about the situation.

      g.   How would you describe yourself (what is your identity?)

h. How do you connect with other systems of which you are a part?

5. Have someone else model the skill and compare your findings with theirs.

6. Now reproduce the thinking and behavior patterns of your subject so that you take on their strategy.

7. Test your model by taking away one element at a time as you use it. If the element isn't key to the process, it won't make any difference. In some cases, taking away an element may even enhance the process. This may take the form of time frames for trading, charting, indicators, preparation for the trading day, preparation for entries and exits, etc.

8. Do the results you achieve match the results your model achieves? If they do, you have been successful. If they don't, go back and find out what other elements make a difference.

9. Note the strategy so that you can continue to use it and, if appropriate, develop it.

Now that we have a firm foundation in modeling, let's examine three other crucial Tools for trading success: Anchoring, Alignment and The Power of Beliefs.

Tools and Techniques Part 1: Anchoring to Support Positive Self-Change

"In any contest between power and patience, bet on patience." - W.B. Prescott

What An Anchor Is And Why It's Important

In college, I was on the track team, and I distinctly remember a very powerful experience during a conference track meet late in the season. It was the end of a long day, the last call for the mile relay, with a slight chill in the spring air and overcast skies. In the stands, a radio played a very loud rendition of "Ain't No Stoppin Us Now". We were, neck and neck for first place with a conference rival with whom we had tangled on more than one occasion during the year. You can imagine how motivated we were to go above and beyond in our individual efforts for the win.

The mile relay was the final meet event and our last chance. My teammate, Steve, and I were making our way to the starting line when the coach told us that Jim, our best quarter miler, was sick and the order of the relay would be changed. Steve, a strong competitor who usually competed in several events during a meet, was picked to run last. He usually ran first. He was the second fastest quarter miler on our team, and had enjoyed a tremendous day, having already won 4 gold metals. The coach switched the order, in case Jim came in behind, so we would have 3 guys to shorten the gap. He put Steve last, figuring his stupendous success that day would give him a slight edge. I was in the 3rd spot and Jason was in the 2nd spot. There were 8 teams in this final's heat, with all the best teams running. The entire team approached the starting line, and the leadoff runner then went to the blocks in his assigned lane. Once the sweats were off and the blocks adjusted, the starter yelled, "ON YOUR MARK!" as a hush settled across the crowd. "GET SET!" The runners raised to a poised position as tension filled the air like a dense fog. "CRACK!" The starter gun pierced the air and the runners exploded from their blocks. Jim ran his heart out, but his illness took its toll and he came in 4th after the first leg. Jason ran an exceptionally strong 2nd leg, made up some ground, and came in 3rd. When I got the baton, I was about 10 yards from number 2 and another 15 yards from the lead runner. I ran my hardest, and still came in 15 yards behind the lead, but I was in the second position. It was now up to Steve. He was up against the conference champ in the quarter mile and the mile. Handing off the baton to Steve, I could see his face showed an unmistakable determination. This was the race of his life. He took the baton and shot off like a canon, catching his rival within the first 120 yards. He then did something unconventional; he passed the leader on the curve, expending more energy than passing on a straight would have required. The leader, knowing this, let him pass and ran in his footsteps, slightly behind, until they came out of the last curve and into the final straight. Steve could feel the other guy pull up alongside him. They were stride for stride. Steve had given just about all he had, but remembered everything coach taught him about the finish—lift the knees high, remain relaxed—and, just as the tape was approaching, Steve flung himself forward to edge out his rival and win the race.

Steve later told me that he could still hear that song, "Ain't No Stoppin Us Now", in his mind. That exuberant, excited and euphoric emotional state of winning was "anchored" for him by that song. From that moment on, that song not only triggered his memory of the events of that day, but also the emotional state associated with that day. As a result, he will "re-experience" what he thought, emotionally felt, and did at that event every time he hears that song.

In order to perform to our capacity, we must manage our "emotional state." This is of critical importance, because emotions can and do gravely impact upon our ability to maintain focus and optimal positive intensity. Any glitch in emotional state leads almost inevitably to a less-than-resourceful response to situations. If we feel irritation, guilt, anger, frustration, doubt, or self-consciousness, we become distracted and fragmented in our effort. In contrast, feelings of ease, confidence, forgiveness, acceptance, inspiration, and amusement are states much more likely to lead us into giving our best, whatever the context.

Different states lend themselves to different circumstances. Some of these states are:

- Thoughtful meditation
- Trust
- Amused self-assurance
- Curious inquisitiveness
- Relaxed intensity
- Controlled exuberance

These are but a few descriptions of countless emotional states that can be as unique as each individual. When we prepare to do anything important, like enter the market, there are emotional states that are supportive and others that are non-supportive. It's important to recognize and choose which states work best for us in those situations and circumstances where our best effort is the only acceptable option. And, once we have the state we want, the challenge is to hold on to it through the potential barrage of circumstances that are out of our control but may trigger a cascade of negative interpretations, like the news event that prompts a market reaction against our position, or the economic report that causes the market to surge erratically both up and down. So it is vitally important that, when these circumstances present themselves, we stand firm and hold on to our convictions and beliefs. Successful traders know how to anchor their emotions and their self-confidence during times of turbulence.

An anchor is a stimulus and can activate a sense like a sound, an image, a touch, a smell, or taste; or it can be a memory that triggers a cascade of internal responses that reflexively alters the state of mind. Anything can be an anchor. This process of anchoring works in both directions to either help or hinder your performance.

The ability to use anchors enables us to:

- Access internal resources like feeling states

- Replace unwanted feelings and thoughts with desirable ones

- Manage emotions

- Remain focused when going through periods of erratic change

- Create the internal experience we prefer, regardless of the environmental circumstances

Anchors act as triggers, and each of us already has a wealth of them, whether positive or negative. Consider the following examples of anchors:

- People close to us

- Memories of seminal events in our lives

- A taste of an extraordinary meal, fine wine or other thing

- A picture or postcard

- A strange touch in a special place on our body

- A astonishing view

- A favorite piece of music

- A special perfume

In an earlier section, I talked about the Results Model. In it, we saw how events are neutral occurrences or circumstances we interpret and to which we give meaning . Events can also be anchors. Consider this:

You get up and one of your children is sick and needs attention. You think about the swing position you are in and the economic report is coming out. You feel a little anxious because you know you'll need to attend to your child, since your wife is leaving for work, and the economic report could negatively affect your position. You've still got some time to take care of the little one and get to your platform. However, you need to call the pediatrician, who rarely is reachable, and you often have to either wait on the phone, or, due to his demeanor, attempt with difficulty to get a word in edgewise and explain what is happening. You find yourself getting irritated with what you consider as time wasters when talking to him. You finally get through the conversation and find it's not serious, but you must go to the pharmacy for special medication for the little one's symptom. On the way, you remember there is construction on the fastest route. You begin to feel tense because the other route takes an extra 15 minutes and it is annoying, since that construction has been going on way too long. And, since you are home alone with the baby, you must get her bundled up to take with you and you feel overwhelmed by the process. When you finally get back and the baby is soundly napping, you realize the report has come and gone and you had not placed a stop. The economic report was not good for your position and you ended up losing more than you were prepared to. The feeling is anger and a knot in your stomach. You notice there is another stock on your watch list that looks poised for a breakout, so you day trade it. You feel like you've got to get your money back, but the play breaks in the opposite direction and is disastrous. You end up losing again and the drawdown has taken a significant amount of your portfolio percentage, because your position size for the intra-day play was more than your rules would allow. Subsequent plays bring similar results and, as the baby awakens, she is crying. You feel overwhelmed, defeated, and with a headache, and you call yourself a schmuck.

On the other hand, consider this:

You get up and one of the children is sick and needs attention. You think about the swing position you are in and the economic report coming out. You feel expectant, but confident, because there is plenty of time to get to your position after you've take care of baby; besides, you'll take a moment to ensure you have a stop in place, in case it goes against you. You've still got some time to take care of the little one and get to your platform for trading. However, you need to call the pediatrician, who rarely is reachable, and you often have to either wait on the phone, or, due to his demeanor, attempt with difficulty to get a word in edgewise and explain what is happening. Taking this into account, you prepare for the phone call by ensuring he gets all the pertinent information upfront and you ensure you have the questions you need answered ready. You finally get through the conversation and find it's not serious, but you must go to the pharmacy for special medication for the little one's symptoms. .On the way, you remember there is construction on the fastest route. As you get the baby bundled to take the trip with you, you put on one of your favorite CD's and think how glad you are that it wasn't serious. When you finally get back and the baby is soundly napping, you realize the report has come and gone and you compliment yourself for remembering to take a moment earlier to place the stop. Since the economic report was not good for your position, you ended up losing much less than you might have. You feel acceptance of the fact that every small loss gets you closer to a big win. You notice there is another stock on your watch list that looks poised for a break-out, so you analyze the data in front of you in a relaxed and focused way, checking it from a number of vantage points before you actually make the trade. You put the other loss behind you and recognize that once a trade is over, you move on and leave it in the past. Once you open a new trade, it is a fresh opportunity to resonate with what is. As a result of being relaxed, you notice something in the data that causes you to exit the trade before it moves into a larger loss, and you feel satisfied that you followed your rules and, therefore, it was a good trade. Your portfolio is down, but not as much as it might have been, since you did not give in to an impulse to put on a larger position than your rules or portfolio warrants. Also, you know you're on track to take advantage of the next high probability opportunity. You shut your platform down, resisting the urge to overtrade. As the baby awakens, she is crying, but you are relaxed and feel able to address her needs in a confident way, just as you negotiated the day. You feel grounded and ready to have a good evening with your spouse once she returns.

Making Anchors Work For You

The associations we have chosen to make, consciously or unconsciously, given the events we face, govern our days. Remember, it is not the neutral event; it is the meaning we ascribe to the event that conjures an emotion which ultimately drives our behavior and then leads to outcomes or results. It boils down to what we are choosing to think about. In this way, we can begin to take control by using anchors hand in hand with results thinking. We can decide how we want to feel, given certain events and situations. For example:

- When we prepare to trade

- When planning a trade

- When entering the market

- When deciding what position size we will initiate

- When the price action breathes

- When something happens unexpectedly

- When the technology upon which we depend fails

- When we are about to exit the market

Anchoring A Resourceful State

The process of anchoring involves linking a specific sound, sight, or touch with an experience. The linking process subsequently enables you to use the anchor to re-access that same experience when it can benefit you in another context.

A procedure for anchoring a resourceful state:

1) Make yourself comfortable in a distraction free space.

2) Identify a powerful state or resource (a feeling) you have experienced in the past and that you'd like to use whenever you choose, like the feeling after a particularly well-played winning trade.

3) Choose an anchor you can use at any time and anywhere to activate that feeling. It must be precise and easy to use. For example, you could make a fist with your dominant hand, or tug on your earlobe with your non-dominant hand, or rub the back of your head with either hand.

4) Now recall the memory or experience where the feeling of empowerment, confidence, relaxation, centeredness, curious, etc., was strongest for you. Make sure you are associated in this experience; that is, you are seeing through your own eyes and in your body. If you can see yourself, this is dissociation, and you won't be able to "feel" your experience if you are looking at yourself outside of your body. You'll need to "feel" the experience in order to "anchor" it. Be sure to experience all of the stimuli in detailed specifics when you have become fully associated into the event. See what is going on around you, vivid colors, whether it is day or night, inside or outside, notice the clothes you are wearing, the shoes on your feet and any other visuals in detail. Be sure to notice the sounds around you. Are they loud or quiet? From what location are they coming? Are people speaking? Are you speaking, and if so, what are you saying? Do the same for any other sense that is/was activated by that experience. Is taste involved? Do you smell anything? Of course, you'll want to apply the same detail to taste and smell that you applied to what you saw, heard, touched or felt. When you have experienced this state and all the senses to as great a degree as possible, then link the chosen anchor, (the clinched fist, the tug on the earlobe, etc.) for as long and only as long as you feel the sensations intensely. When you have experienced the state

and the tug on the earlobe, release the touch, shake yourself or move in some way to "break state."

5) You have now initiated an anchor with this touch for the feelings you want. You will want to repeat this process several times until you know there is a strong connection between the touch and the feeling.

6) To test the anchor, think of something else and, as you do, tug on your earlobe in precisely the same manner as when linking the touch and the feeling. This is called "Firing the anchor." If done correctly, you will re-experience the anchored event with all of the attending sensory-rich memory state. If this does not occur, keep practicing. You may not have been fully associated when you set the anchor. Make sure you used the same process of touching used to recall the experience as you did to set it up. Also, ensure you set the anchor just as the feelings are at their highest degree, and take it away just as it wanes or fades away.

7) Now go into the future and conjure up a situation you think the anchor would be helpful in activating. As you imagine the future situation, fire the anchor. After you've done so, notice what you are experiencing, seeing, hearing, and feeling. This is especially effective for trading scenarios where you have noticed extraordinary fear and greed invariably accompanied by impulsive and compulsive behavior. This process is useful when you have incorporated your journal entries to identify the instances where you have noticed swells of these unproductive emotions and feeling states. Self-discipline is supported not by hard-nosed will, but by the passion of our emotions as we tie the intensity of positive emotions to the behaviors we know are supportive of the results we desire.

Chaining Resources

Now that you've learned how to activate resourceful feeling states to support your optimal performance, it is only a small step further to learn how to address some of the deep seated and particularly difficult feeling states that may require a "chain" of anchors to shuttle you from the least resourceful state to one strongly associated with the results you want. An example is going from a profoundly fragmented and anxious state, like one brought on by an automobile accident or a profound drawdown, to a centered, accepting and focused state. You might transition through a gradient of states that would gradually move you from anger, to concern, to neutrality, to acceptance, to release, to relaxation. This is chaining anchors in a way that progressively moves you from distressful states to one that is optimal. Practicing this process is a sure-fire way to be on a trajectory to achieving goals.

1) Decide on an unsupportive state. Then choose a state that is significantly different, presumably polar opposite to the first state. For instance, you might identify fear as one end and unbridled confidence as the other.

2) Access the state of fear by remembering a sensory rich experience; that is, see, hear, smell, touch and taste as many details that were available in the original event. Associate with it by "feeling" it in your own body. Then anchor it by rubbing your chin. Then break state by clapping your hands or taking a step backward.

3) Access the next shuttle state, for example mild anxiety. This, of course, would be of less intensity than the fear. Access this feeling by remembering a time when you experienced anxiety, for instance, when looking at the tick move against you. When you have fully associated

into it, anchor it by touching your nose with the same hand and finger(s). Then break state.

4) Choose a more supportive state, for instance, safety. Then associate into the experience of safety and anchor it by touching your temple. When you have done this successfully, break state.

5) The number of steps you must take will depend on the intensity of the original state and the gap between it and the desired state. Repeat this process until you have anchored all of the intermediate states and the final state.

6) Test the anchors and make sure you break state after each state. If needed, return to any that are not fully anchored.

7) At this point, you are ready to fire all the anchors in sequence. For instance, suppose there are 5 going from fear (chin – right index finger) to anxiety (nose – left index finger) to safety (cheek – right index finger) to confidence (forehead – left index finger). As each state is fired and experienced to the greatest degree, move to the next anchor as you experience the peak while continuing to hold the previous anchor. You should experience each state as they are fired and, as you do, you are connecting them together in a chain. Do this until you have experienced the desired state; then fully remove the previous anchor and feel the final desired state. Then break state. Be sure to break state after each practice of the chain to ensure a loop with the original state is not inadvertently created.

8) Repeat step 7 until you have the states chained together.

9) Fire the first anchor. If you have been successful, the chain will fire as well and all of the states will sequentially express through your body.

This process can and does manifest spontaneously in our lives just by habit and routine. However, because most people are not aware of this level of detail in their lives, the process takes longer to manifest or the individual gets looped back into undesirable states. How often have you seen a trade set-up and you made a mistake in execution, only to then experience frustration, then irritation, then anger and stress, and then to find yourself distracted and ineffective with the rest of your trades during that session? Wouldn't it be much more empowering to find that, if you do get into a state of frustration, it can lead to inquisitiveness, introspection, increased awareness and a learning moment that can be used in the next opportunity to attract more desired results? If mastered, this process is a vital tool in creating paradigm shifts in both insight and overall effectiveness, because you are learning to recognize opportunities to control feeling states and thereby control your behavior.

Anchoring Insight

For each of us, there comes moments when we "rise above" and exhibit stellar performance. It might be associated with sports, business, interrelationships or of course trading. During these times, we bring together quite well what we have learned, and in addition to the skill we exhibit, there is an accompanying feeling state encompassing all the encoded thought and behavioral sequences that went into the performance. Unfortunately, these moments often go unheeded by our consciousness. That is not to say we don't know when we've done a good job, but if asked, many would not be able to detail exactly what they thought, felt and did to achieve their results . However, when they do and can bring up to consciousness the process in a way that can be replicated—that is called insight. Insight depends upon our ability to become aware of environmentally teachable

---

moments. This is how change is achieved and accelerated, by becoming first consciously competent and then practicing that skill set until it becomes unconsciously competent.

Do you remember when you were about 5 or 6 years old and everyone climbed into the family car to go somewhere? You were unconsciously incompetent about driving. You didn't know how to drive nor were you conscious that you didn't know. When you were about 12 or 13, you became "aware" that this automobile device was something that provided "freedom" and you became painfully aware that you didn't know how to drive, but you wanted to learn some day. You then became consciously incompetent; you knew you didn't know. At some point, you began to learn and, if you learned on a stick shift, there invariably came a time you found yourself at the top of a hill with a red light that looked the size of a crimson sun staring you in the face, and although you were taught how to negotiate the clutch, brake, gas and stick shift, you were required to think about each step in the sequence—much to the ire of the long line of cars that let their horns do the talking as you were sweating bullets while the car kept stalling out. You knew, but couldn't apply, the knowledge competently. Even though you could be described as consciously competent, you knew that you knew, but you had to think about each move.

To state the obvious, if you don't know something then it doesn't exist for you. Often our improveables remain as such because they are beyond our awareness. In order for us to change, we must first become aware, and we have discussed the importance of journaling to help support that process. This is another process structure that will help you manage and facilitate change, i.e., anchoring insight—the process of gaining an "aha" about empowerment states that can then be incorporated into your tool box, practiced and assimilated into an unconscious way of doing and performing to achieve the desired results.

For instance, sometimes when you are trading, you have followed your rules, practiced appropriate money management and position sizing and, through adroit analysis, have been in sync with the market and were able to extract a very nice profit. This process is a way to replicate the state and therefore the skill sets associated with it to become unconsciously competent with this tool:

1) Decide on a trigger you want to use the next time you experience a state you want to anchor (a touch, word, or image you activate).

2) Give yourself an internal alarm the next time you experience a desirable state (which could be unexpected so you get a prompt to anchor it). This could be done by asking your unconscious mind to remind you with a thought of anchoring the next time you are in a desirable resource state.

3) When you are at the height of the desirable state, use your anchor to "stamp" or encode it.

4) If it happens repeatedly, use your anchor each time you are at the height of the emotions to strengthen the effect of the anchor.

5) Think of occasions when the state you have just anchored might be useful to you.

6) The next time you are in a situation when you feel this state that you have anchored might be useful, fire the anchor.

Tools and Techniques Part 2: Alignment

"Destiny is no matter of chance. It is a matter of choice: It is not a thing to be waited for, it is a thing to be achieved" - William Jennings Bryant

Internal and External Congruency

When we think, feel, say, and do in a way that is congruent—meaning that we have internal and external consistency, perceived by others as sincerity or authenticity—then we are in alignment. It can also be termed an 'intra-rapport', moving in tandem with self, in sync and balanced, centered and grounded. We can also be described as having integrity and 'walking our talk'. Alignment cannot be overstated, for like a wheel alignment, or the congruency and alignment of the moving parts of an engine or piece of machinery, if integrity and alignment are compromised, even in minute ways, the object will either not reach its destination or it will, due to wear, become off course and disengaged to the point of disruption and destruction. On the other hand, when alignment is true, optimal performance is all but guaranteed. All parts are moving towards the same goal with precision.

Have you ever tried to ride a bicycle with loose or uneven wheels? They begin to wobble, the gears don't shift optimally, and the brakes rub, causing severe resistance and even immobility. Humans are often out of alignment, but sadly, many don't recognize it. They trudge along trying through force of will to achieve desired outcomes, and when they descend into mental and emotional fatigue due to the stress of moving against themselves, they often wonder why and search for the answer to their issues from every vantage point but the one that matters—inside of themselves.

Some of the more important parts involved in being aligned are:

- Purpose

- Beliefs

- Values

- Identity

- Capability

- Behavior

- Environment

Purpose (previously discussed as Step 1 in the 7 Secrets of Self-Disciplined Trading) is first on this list because it's of vital importance that you've identified the reason why you are in pursuit of any goal, objective, desire. You must be able to answer the "why" question. A compelling reason will not only move, but catapult you to achievement. There are categories of reasons that form the context for being compelling, such as:

Marriage or family—when we associate the thing we want with the people we cherish, that thing we want also inherits a large degree of that energy. The reasons might be spiritual in nature by tying it to your notion of the Creator and devotion; that is, to do things on a higher plane. Also, the concept of community or the planet and one's desire to be an agent for positive change would be a powerful reason as well. Or, the reasons may have a strong tie with personal growth. Knowing the underlying substantive reasons why you want to invest or trade greatly supports your success. Know what your purpose is for investing/trading and any other important endeavor.

Belief Systems

Next, it's significant as well to have a belief system in keeping with your purpose. You must know what your beliefs are. If you believe you lack the intelligence and analytical skills, or if you think that the markets are based on "luck" and you are not lucky, then it doesn't matter much how compelling your reason is. You are out of sync and the prospects of becoming successful—as long as you harbor those notions—are slim to none. As mentioned in the sections on belief, you should be able to answer the question: What are my beliefs about the market, my abilities, my worthiness?

Values

Values are also critical. As with beliefs, values must, for the most part, be uncovered. You may want to "choose" values that are lofty and noble, but if you aren't already "living" a value, it is not a personal value; it's a personal principle, no matter how much you espouse it. Personal principles and values are similar but not the same. Personal principles are what you hold as important, and you aim to be true to those standards and maintain them. Personal principles of living are what you want to live by. Values are how you are living. Once you identify a personal principle and incorporate it into your life by committing to it as a standard, using it as a mantra of movement, then you transition to holding it as a value. That is why values-clarification is misunderstood by some. They think that, given a list of salient-sounding concepts like honesty, charity, health, wisdom, learning, diligence, integrity and so forth, they would then include in their personal values list the ones they "like." However, you can no more declare a value than you can declare good health without doing what it takes to be in good health; this would be out of alignment and incongruent. You would have to declare your commitment to good health, then eat, sleep, and exercise to finish the equation to take it from personal principle or aim to a personally held value. Personal principles are chosen; values are discovered. You can change a principle into a value once it is assimilated into the fabric of your being and reflected in how you live. So, true personal values are reflected in where your attention flows and your behavior shows. There are numerous values-clarification exercises designed to help you identify what your true values are. I would strongly suggest that, if you haven't already, you walk, don't run, to your nearest clarification module and use it to first *find*, then (through other programs suggested in this book) *recalibrate* your values to reflect where you want to go as opposed to where you've been.

Universal Principles

Then there are universal principles. Universal principles are those fundamental and classical truths that are abiding, deep, unwavering and, according to Stephen Covey, "generic common denominators..." tightly interwoven threads running with exactness, consistency, beauty, and strength through the fabric of life. They don't get mad and treat us differently. They won't divorce us or run away with our best friend. They aren't out to get us. They can't pave our way with shortcuts and quick fixes. They don't depend on the behavior of others, the environment, or the current fad for their validity. Universal principles don't die. They aren't here one day and gone the next. They can't be destroyed by fire, earthquake or theft. Values can be personal principles, the difference is a qualitative." [insert name of publication from which this quote was taken]

Identity

Identity is the description of who you are. Of course, we must first figure out which person in *you* we're talking about. Who are you first thing in the morning? Who are you when you are really stressed? Who are you when things are going well? Who are you when you've just entered into a trade with an oversized position? The fact of the matter is that we are not one personality; rather, we are an amalgam of any number of personas fashioned by our experiences taken from all manner of influential figures throughout our lives. The trick is to identify the person you'd like to be and begin to incorporate courageous change works into your daily routine to activate the strong, healthy parts of you. In this way, you can use the treasure from your wounds and focus on the goals of your highest and best self. When you are able to do this, you are on your way to becoming, step by step, the person you aspire to be.

Mission

Mission is connected with Identity in that the mission drives the 'who' you espouse to be. For instance, I have a family and friends mission, a work mission, a play mission, a business mission, and a trading mission. A mission might be to "participate in the markets and be successful in personal terms and as a community partner." My mission and motto is "helping people grow." It encapsulates the picture that is driven by my purpose.

My purpose, mission and aim is multifold and includes:

- To remain connected in each moment of everyday with the Infinite Spirit Whose Omniscient Power of Light and Love Energy is inside me.

- To remain connected with family, friends and all other light beings as I move in HER presence.

- To fully accept and express exactly who I am, a child, emissary and heir of the Mother/Father's Eternal Love and Blessings.

- To accept and express the important roles of my life with unbridled enthusiasm, confidence and effectiveness.

- To accept and express that I have infinite good and share fully my infinite bounty.

- To express this Divine Power through the development and highly successful application of all my talents, assets and abilities.

- To manifest and communicate a message of healing love throughout the planet and planes.

- To remain an open and clear conduit of electrifying growth energy for all who enter into my aura.

- To laugh uncontrollably, to love unconditionally, to live uncompromisingly and to learn continuously.

Capabilities, in this sense, don't have as much to do with what you are capable of at this moment as they do with what you are building capacity to accomplish in the future. However, every person has a set of strengths, improveables and limitations. Get to know them intimately. I love to laugh, but my current strength is not in telling jokes; in fact, I'm so poor at it that people have gotten annoyed with me. I like people, but can't remember names. Obviously, if I wanted to be a well liked comedian, it might be an uphill battle. I would first need to identify what improveables were critical to the goal, what strengths were supportive and a change strategy that would address all of the critical mass issues so that my capabilities would then be in line with the desired outcome. What are my trading strategies and what is my trading profile?

What are you doing? Are you focused with a purpose that encompasses the desired outcome? Behaviors are the test of alignment. In other words, are you doing what you said you were going to do, like keeping commitments, following through with projects and following up on task items? Do you have a trading plan and are you following through on it? Do you have trading rules? Are you practicing appropriate money management and position sizing? When you have losses or experience other disappointments, are you able to accept the reality and move on, or do you wallow in self-pity, sadness, and anger? Are you following the market? Or, do you wish, hope, pray, and otherwise try to make the market go where you want it to go? Are you journaling? Are you logging your trades? What you do speaks volumes about who you are. Alignment also relates to how you are conducting yourself in other parts of your life. For example, are you laughing (the true universal elixir)? Are you expecting more from others than you are willing to give yourself? Are you keeping your promises? Are you having difficult conversations with loved ones and other important people in your life? Are you exhibiting courage?

Remaining In And Going Out Of Alignment

"Remaining in alignment" has to do with first knowing where you are and, secondly, where you want to go; in other words, having a vision of the results you want. Remaining in alignment also presumes you already are in alignment, possessing a sense of self, an understanding of who you are in relationship to whom you want to be. It involves saying what you mean and meaning what you say. It is supremely difficult to achieve results in direct contradiction to what you are thinking and doing. In other words, to say you want to be in great physical condition when you rarely exercise and continually tell yourself that you'll "get around to it" is a prescription for major internal conflict. Part of the question lies in how large your comfort zone is. Small comfort zones ensure that unsupportive emotional states will abound, for instance, anxiety, fear, trepidation, apprehension, guilt, sadness, anger, irritation, annoyance, self-doubt, self-loathing, and self-pity, to name a few. These unsupportive emotional states create disturbances and distraction, rob focus and concentration, and send ripples of mind/body quakes through the system that continually create internal conflict and immobilization. The concept of expansion-of-comfort-zone directly relates to your ability to "disobey" internal restrictions and learned limitations that have mentally and emotionally imprisoned you. The baby elephant tethered by a rope to a stake therefore grows up to be a controllable behemoth because it has been trained to believe it can't get away. This has happened through the conflict that arises when the desired result is out of alignment with the internal beliefs or mythology. This "gap" causes mental anguish and emotional pain as experienced by the above unsupportive emotional states. What exists then is a victim to the internal mythology, which can be especially insidious if the belief system is unconscious or out of awareness. Part of expanding your comfort zone means becoming conscious—that is, beginning to become aware of what you don't know about yourself.

Limiting internal feeling states are like your own internal prison guards. Disobeying internal prison guards means thinking for yourself and becoming "creatively curious" about your intentions and underlying mythology. You will want to question your limiting concepts by personal appreciative inquiry into your thoughts and behaviors. For instance, some people believe they must have a job in order be productive and worthy, or "Before I can work, I must have a job," or "Before I can make money I must have money," or "I need to make money before I can be a somebody and worthy of another's esteem." These and countless others may be lurking inside the mind of your internal prison guard— the part of you that has been entrusted to keep you "safe." The aligned person reframes these self-limiting and sabotaging statements by saying, for instance, "I

---

don't need a job to work. I can find out what others need and want, produce it, and get them to pay me or it," or " I know that many others have done what I want to do and they do not have any more intelligence, drive, or creativity than I." To some, these statements amount to a paradigm shift of thinking and doing, and that is what it takes for most of us to reframe, redirect and reprogram the "mental prison guard" into an internal ally that no longer is overly invested in safety, but now is invested in vitality and thriving through the adventure of life. However, even when the prison guards have been neutralized, they can fall prey to a "reversal" when we are met with adversity (loss, threat, stress, pain, etc.).

Steps To Personal Congruence

Another concept in Stephen Covey's *7 Habits of Highly Successful People* is "proactive vs. reactive," that is, to anticipate issues through becoming aware of improveables and making pre-emptive movements. Most people only put this principle to work when situations or external circumstances throw an obstacle at them they can't avoid or escape. Even when external circumstances throw the curve ball, it's nice to be able to see it coming—but that's the easy one. It's much more difficult to get out of the behavioral rut or the internal challenge due to the conflict it presents. Being proactive means we are actively working on uncovering those demons and actively addressing them as well. But when the demons hit, they are more likely to get stuck in what Robert Fritz calls the "reactive-response orientation" (*The Path of Least Resistance*) as opposed to the "creative orientation." The "reactive-response" is constrictive, narrow, and self-limiting behavior that has at its emotional foundation anxiety and fear. The "creative orientation" is expansive, flexible and curious. A self-actualizing, conscious decision-maker actively seeks out opportunities to do new and different things. It's damn difficult to swim against the tide of old habits, especially when they are accompanied, as they often are, by strong fear and/or greed. So as you step outside your comfort zone, you could do the following:

---

1) Recognize the mechanism; in other words, identify what happens in your thought process when you attempt to override the urge to do or not do that which creates the issue-- for instance, placing a trade that has a 10% risk of capital when your rule is 2%. This is facilitated by journaling the process, thoughts and feelings, as soon as it happens.

2) Notice how much more effectively you handle the obstacle when you do so from the creative orientation rather than from the reactive-responsive orientation. The creative orientation might be to try something different, to present a "pattern interrupt" when the conflict happens. This is decidedly difficult and requires courage and being fully present and in the moment. But it is doable. For instance, try standing, singing out loud, taking a deep breath, or dropping down to do 20 push-ups. It needs to be something that "breaks the state." The reactive-responsive orientation might be to shut down the curious part of you, go into trance, and by splitting into disparate intentions and "mindlessly" allow the urge to take over, or while held hostage by the habit, to tell yourself the story of how "it's going to work this time."

3) Notice that every time you successfully handle and overcome the wayward rascal inside or the unaligned intention driven by fear or greed, you become more capable of dealing with negativity in general. Your comfort zone expands and rises. You build capacity and strength to resist the urge, and more importantly, remain grounded, centered and aligned while in the moment of the decision rather that thinking later about how you could have done it better after experiencing the pain of the loss.

4) Learn that you can deliberately engage the creativity orientation by exercising courage and by consciously choosing to do things outside your comfort zone. It isn't easy, but if it were, you would not be reading this book.

Tools and Techniques Part 3: The Power of Beliefs

Beliefs of Excellence

"Each problem that I solved became a rule which served afterwards to solve other problems." - Rene Descartes (1596-1650), *Discours de la Methode*

We spoke earlier about the importance of beliefs. In this section, we will delve a little deeper to identify ways to "use" the power of beliefs as a tool. We become what we truly believe and we've all heard the quote, "The thought is father to the deed." Whatever your beliefs are, the first matter of business is to know them, especially those that impact your life and trading performance. It is best to be clear about them by listing those at your center, and valuable to engender a belief in excellence. A belief in excellence is about what is at the core of success-- your success; and with regard to those beliefs (either conscious or unconscious), either you are living them, learning them or you are losing. Winning is about belief. If you believe you can't, you won't; if you believe you can, you might. If passion is fire, then emotionally connected beliefs are the logs that build that bonfire of focus on the goal.

Beliefs are also emotionally held thoughts based on our perceptions of events. Consider trying on a new suit of clothes. Let's say you can have them as long as you want, so you can try them on for fit, feel, comfort, and look. Also, you may be interested in the reactions of others. Because clothes are interchangeable, even if you look great in the jacket and pants or skirt but not the shirt, tie or blouse, you can keep what you like and take the rest back. What you keep might be worn with your other clothes. Beliefs are like this-- you can presuppose they are truth and you can try them on. If they work, it is likely they will become a belief. If not, you can disregard them.

Beliefs influence all behavior. Here is a list of proactive beliefs:

- There are no failures, only lessons

- Every problem has a solution

- I have everything within me that I need

- Everyone is unique

- Creativity is at my core, and I can always try something different

- Mind and body are part of the same system

- Knowledge is not power, the application of knowledge is power

- All that I need to know is either inside of me or available to me

- If I am patient, there is always another trade

- I don't have to always participate in the market

- The market is made of people like me, therefore if I can determine my poor decisions I can take the other side of the trade with a high probability of being right

How Beliefs Originate

I know a woman named Amber. She is a well adjusted and successful businesswoman and trader; however, she had considerable difficulties when she first began to trade. She earned a PhD in college and her nose-to-the-grindstone attitude helped her excel in business, but worked to her detriment in trading. She experienced herself wanting to trade the way she worked: endlessly, putting many deliverables on her plate at once, and barreling through her workday. She said she liked her day this way because it gave her an edge, but when she employed this same tactic to her trading, she had dismal results and it almost depleted all of her capital. She knew there had to be something driving her thinking and creating such depressing results. After working with her journal and engaging in some deep introspection, she realized that, when faced with doing things the easy way versus the hard or difficult way, she had chosen, time and time again, the difficult path. It had never occurred to her this could be an issue, and during graduate school and business, things had always come out the way she wanted. One day, while speaking to her mentor about her trading, she remembered something her Dad used to tell her: "Amber, you always do things the hard way." She also remembered becoming angry and hurt by his admonition and realized she had, in fact, chosen to be that way throughout her life. She *believed* she had to do things the hard way because she *believed* that was her way. With the uncovering of that belief she then resolved to change her way of thinking by reframing the belief into one that served her. Subsequently, she changed her behavior in order to get the results she wanted.

Beliefs are MAPS and serve to create views about self and others that determine decisions. These beliefs and MAPS, if they do not serve us, are learned limitations that become "dyed-in-the-wool" and strongly held, often coming from authority figures and loved ones we incorporated into our maps.

Consider how wounding and destructive beliefs like the following can be:

- You're a dummy

- You'll never amount to much

- You deserve everything that you get

- You're a bad seed

- Children should be seen and not heard

- You're lazy

- People can't be trusted

- Rich people do bad things

- You've got to get all you can before it is taken away

- Only greedy people have money

You can create your own beliefs and rewrite your history. It is a matter of identifying the results you want and formulating the mindset aligned with getting those results.

Consider the following:

Jim is an excellent trader. He knows how to trade and he believes whole-heartedly in his ability to do what it takes to win. Even though he knows losing is part of trading, he treats each play as though he is definitely going to capture money from the market.

1) Belief – I have the potential to win any trade I make

2) I follow all of my rules and size my positions appropriately. I manage my portfolio.

3) I only take high probability setups in keeping with my strategy.

4) I'm able to visualize the winning trade as hitting my target. I can see the price action moving in my favor. I see myself smiling as I click the mouse to enter and to exit the winning trade. I hear myself say, "well done" after the winning.

5) I feel confident and am aligned with my strengths while resisting disruptive emotions like anxiety, fear and greed.

6) I put my full attention into the trade. I am focused and the "knowledgeable trader" in me is fully present.

7) I look for patterns, pivots, resistance and support and use them adroitly.

8) I notice when I have "danced with the market well" and celebrate my wins.

9) I prove my belief to myself by taking advantage of good high probability set-ups that have a high rate of win returns.

How Beliefs Influence Our Lives

"He who hesitates is a damned fool." - Mae West (1892-1980)

If on the other hand, Jim believed he had to fight the market, and it was difficult to win, and that at any moment the markets would take his money, the scenario would be more like the one below.

1) Belief – beating the market is difficult and I don't have much of a chance. Winners are lucky.

2) My rules don't really matter that much. I need to make money when I can. If I play more, I can make more.

3) I take advice wherever I can get it and take any and all set-ups. I've got to remain flexible. If I don't I'll miss out.

4) I hope that this trade will win. If I anticipate the move of the price action, I can get a jump on the trade, but I know it's going to go against me as soon as I get in, and when I get a small profit I'd better take it now because the price action will move against me.

5) I'm feeling anxious and fearful that I'm going to lose.

6) I know it's going to break out of resistance, so I'll go long early. I don't need confirmation. If I wait, I'll miss part of the move.

7) I feel like a failure when I've lost in a trade.

8) I prove my belief to myself.

This scenario plays out over and over again in trading rooms and on computers across the planet. Be proactive and intentional about your belief systems. This is the way to create the results in your life and in your trading that you want.

Achieving the Results You Want

"If everything seems under control, you're just not going fast enough." -Mario Andretti

Problem Thinking

Jack experienced a massive drawdown on his portfolio. This is not the first time; in fact, he has experienced a string of loses over the past several months. He has taken course after course, but it seems he just can't make it happen. However, he has realized his money management could be much better. He has found himself in countless positive trades only to exit at the wrong time. He has taken small profits only to have big losers wipe them out. He knows he's got to do something about this.

Jordan likes to think of himself as a swing trader, and he enjoys trading options. He has several trading buddies who are day traders in Futures and Forex. They have told him on many occasions that he could do so much better in these markets. Jordan has tried them but every time he finds something goes wrong, he misses late night trades in Forex because he is not a night person, or he gets bored sitting in front of a screen for hours at a time the way his buddies do. But he feels he is not doing well enough and his options trades are doing so much better. He feels dissatisfied in the same arenas as his friends.

Jack and Jordan both are caught in problem thinking. They are immersed in the *issue* rather that focused on what they truly want. Jack has issues with emotional control and exercising appropriate money management, but he is caught in the cycle of impulsive and compulsive behavior. Jordan is not oriented strongly enough to his style. He allows others to dissuade him from what he enjoys, and as a result is left feeling less than and not good enough. They are both focused on the problem or, in other words, on the "current reality" rather than "future reality."

Achieving desired results is like sailing to England from New York. You'll never get there if you're focused on not sailing to Tahiti. You need to know where you want to end up before you set sail. This is one of the predominant issues with individuals who find themselves in a perceived vicious circle and feeling as if they are failures. It's important to know what you really want and to make that desired thing the focus of your endeavors. The difference between those who achieve what they want and those who merely engage in wishful thinking is that achievers have an ability to be prepared to pay the price, which often means letting everything go so they can achieve what they really want. The things we believe we cannot do without are often the very same things we need to let go of if we are to realize our deepest desires.

People who achieve what they want in life have compelling goals. There is a pattern to the structure of their thinking around their goals, of which they are usually unaware. This is not about what you must, should, or ought to do. Nor is it about what you don't want to do or what you will try to do. Those kinds of thoughts tend to be precipitates of the goals that others want for you rather than those outcomes and results that you truly want for yourself. Results orientation is thinking about what you really *do* want. That may seem selfish, but we cannot make others' goals come true for them. Although we do influence others, it is really about what we achieve for ourselves.

Ask yourself the question: What do I really want:

- Today?

- Tomorrow?

- This year?

- Next year?

- In the next five years?

- In my career?

- In my life?

Thinking of what you don't want is problem thinking. It focuses on what you want to change—even though it seems logical to focus on what and how you want to change something. This leads to "away from" thinking, meaning you are motivated away from that which you don't want. You might move to a new house to get away from the area in which you lived; you might have changed jobs because your boss or co-workers were not to your liking; or you might change brokers because you didn't like the structure of the broker you were using. This kind of goal might be expressed like this:

- I want to stop drinking so much alcohol

- I want to stop smoking

- I want to lose this fat stomach

- I must clean my garage

- I want to stop feeling so much fear in my trades

- I have to stop losing so much money

- I have to reduce the amount of stress in my life

These are examples of thinking of the condition you are in, even though you want to change them.

Sharon has been trading for only a year. She understands she is lacking important knowledge and is willing to do what it takes to get the knowledge she needs. She also realizes she is at a disadvantage and that the first order of business is to protect her portfolio at all costs. She is fiercely attuned to what is in her best interests, and she passionately wants to achieve her stated goals. She talks to her trading buddies about what is important to her and about how to accomplish goals for herself and others. She is respectful of differences of opinion but is not easily moved from her objectives. Her eyes are on the prize. People are drawn to her and she seems well grounded, centered and full of life.

What precisely is the difference in the way Sharon thinks about her results and the way Jack and Jordan think about theirs? Sharon certainly seems to be on track to achieve her outcome and is enjoying the journey toward it.

Outcome Thinking or Results Orientation

Results orientation is about envisioning what you really want as if you stepped into the future and got it. This is towards thinking moving proactively towards what you want by beginning with the end in mind. For instance, moving to a new house because you found that perfect one you wanted; moving to a new job because you loved the opportunity; or identifying what you want in a broker and finding those features in one and making the move. Another is exercising to be fit, reducing stress because you enjoy feeling relaxed and focused, or cleaning the garage because you truly enjoy having storage space and being organized. Consider the difference:

- I want to be in good health

- I want to be strong and physically fit

- I want a clean and organized garage

- I want to be in control of my emotions when I trade

- I want to exercise good money management

- I want to enjoy greater happiness and centeredness in my life

Moving toward a goal creates focus by increasing the energy around the desired condition; your energy flows where your attention goes. Consider the statement: "Don't think about an elephant!" For most people, this suggestion is impossible to follow. Your subconscious mind has difficulty recognizing negatives. When you tell yourself not to worry or not to make a mistake, you are actually programming yourself to do just that. However, if you program yourself to think about being calm or getting things right, you are dramatically increasing the chances, this is how you will be.

Achievers, especially sports figures or other physical performance oriented individuals, have mastered self-programming. They know if they are on the tee or the green and they let their thoughts wander to "not" choking, that is exactly what will happen. They know if they start worrying about hitting the ball out of the court, that is what they are programming themselves to do. Even if the bulk of their thinking is positive, they know a fleeting negative thought can make the difference between winning the point and losing it. They have modeled themselves on excellence.

How often have you said to yourself, "I mustn't do that" only to find yourself doing it? Jack, in the above example, told himself when the price action is accelerating on volume to be careful and breath when he wants to enter and "Don't enter until the candle closes." Well, the very next time he gets into that situation, what do you think he will do? He enters as soon as he sees the candle beginning to blast off and gets filled at the top only to see it decline way back down right after he enters.

Results-oriented-thinking is about identifying what galvanizes your focus and your passion. It is about creating a sensory-rich vision of success around which you can build the fire of desire for what makes your heart sing. In other words, identifying that which you "really want."

Trading is a purely mental game, and if you don't fully recognize and appreciate that, you are tossing your fate to serendipity, and you are gambling. And we all know what happens to gamblers in the long run. In the next section, we will explore one of the most effective ways to establish and sustain results oriented thinking.

Emotional Field Technique

"The real voyage of discovery consists not in seeking new lands but seeing with new eyes." - Marcel Proust

Emotional Freedom Technique is a powerful approach to personal change-work that is among the fastest and most effective non-invasive procedures for addressing intra-psychic and/or physical issues. Successful trading requires emotional control and behavioral follow-through. By implementing a fairly simple and brief protocol, substantial progress can be made in honing effectiveness in areas where demonstrated excellent results have been achieved, including:

Emotional Challenges:

- Reduction of stress and anxiety
- Control of internal responses to fear and greed
- Stabilization of anger and frustration
- Depression
- Fears and phobias
- Negative memories and inner child issues
- Self-doubt

Health Issues:

- Reduction of substance cravings

- Pain relief

- Weight loss

- General well-being

Increased Overall Effectiveness:

- Improved mental flexibility and focus

- Improved ability to sustain keeping commitment

- Improved performance in sports, career, concentration

- Control of impulsive and compulsive behavior

- Release of learned limitations about internal relationships to money and wealth

- Improved business and personal relationships

- Improved assertiveness

- ·Enhanced personal and spiritual growth processes

- Building courage for new endeavors

EFT was created by Gary Craig and Adrienne Fowlie in the mid 1990's, and is meant to be a simplification and improvement of Dr. Roger Callahan's Thought Field Therapy techniques (a process using the meridians of acupuncture and energy flow). Acupuncture is a traditional Chinese medical technique for unblocking chi (chi or qi) by inserting needles at particular points on the body to balance the opposing forces of yin and yang. Chi is an energy that purportedly permeates all things. It is believed to flow through the body along 14 main pathways called meridians. When yin and yang are in harmony, chi flows freely within the body and a person is healthy. When a person is sick, diseased, or injured, there is an obstruction of chi along one of the meridians.

Craig trained with Callahan in the early 1990s. In 1993, Craig was the first person Callahan trained in his most advanced procedure, a proprietary procedure known as Voice Technology. This technology consisted of protocols of tapping along specific meridian in specific sequences depending upon the issue(s) that were being addressed. Craig found through his experience that the sequence of tapping points did not matter and that special proprietary procedures were therefore unnecessary, so by the mid-1990s he had simplified Callahan's procedures. It is numbered among other non-traditional psychotherapeutic theories known collectively as Energy Psychology.

For purposes of this discussion, tapping on meridian points to cleanse the flow of emotional disruption and constipation facilitates emotional energy flow. Dr. Callahan calls it "psychological reversal." The concept of "psychological reversal" can arguably be identified as the root of many issues and challenges that plague the average woman and man, although attempting to get their life in order, the messes keep coming back in spades. Look at trading. Over and over again, you have fallen prey to many of the same mistakes, pitfalls and brick walls you've said over and over you would not. As the saying goes, fool me once, shame on you; fool me twice, shame on me. Many of us have been fooled so many times we have our own fool's cap. But what's the real perpetrator inside you? Well, it seems that shock, trauma, or repeated lessons can cause the energy flow relating to a particular subject to become reversed; i.e., it does the opposite of what you want it to do. For example, most people have one or more, or a single massive reversal on, health related issues. If they were muscle-tested they would test weak on "I want to be healthy," which means they don't believe it, and for them, that is not actually true at all. For those not familiar with muscle testing, it is an applied kinesiology procedure using a phrase or thought repeated while "testing" the muscle. For instance, the arm may be tested while repeating the phrase. If the phrase or thought is believed, the muscle responds with strength; if it is not believed, the muscle responds with weakness.

These are the people who struggle endlessly with substance addictions—weight and fitness problems and, of course, highly challenging endeavors like trading the financial markets. These are the people who are trying to fight themselves using "willpower" to overcome their own internal programming that runs to the reverse of what everyone—including parts of themselves—are telling them they "should" or "should not" be doing.

Clinical psychologist, Dr. Roger Callahan, founder and developer of the Callahan Techniques® Thought Field Therapy, writes in *The Origins of Psychological Reversal*:

"Any form of psychological reversal appears to be rooted in a deep rejection of self on the part of the individual. Reversed people do not believe they **deserve** to succeed. They consider themselves unworthy of good things and deserving of failure and unhappiness. Dr. Albert Ellis dubbed this syndrome the "worthless piece of shit" approach to life. A person suffering from this condition considers himself so valueless that he deserves no happiness or success in life. I have found that this condition can exist in many degrees.

One person may feel very positive and deserving in many areas of his life and worthless in only one specific field. Another individual may be suffering from a negative image of himself in every area of his life. The more extensive the psychological reversal, the more difficult it is to treat and, generally, the more often it needs to be dealt with."

EFT is easy, almost effortless, and works quickly. Emotions are like frequencies of energy that can be debilitating; for example, anxiety, fear, unchecked exuberance and greed. These murder your trading success, but can be reduced or neutralized in a short time, often within a single session, or several sessions over a few weeks, compared to months or years of traditional therapy. The process is so simple and takes such a small amount of time, it is conceivable to use the technique before every trade initially. By doing this, you greatly decrease the negative emotions hindering your ability to see reality, while increasing focus and an overall ability to "dance" with the markets in real time. Staying on the "winning" side of the order flow will be easier, thereby creating more success.

As with your general trading, keeping a journal of your personal development alongside your trading is highly advised. In their book, *Getting Thru to Your Emotions,* Jane and Phillip Mountrose give the following advise:

- Stay Focused – record goals and successes and note things you'll want to remember later.

- Record New Levels of Awareness – like anything, new awareness is subject to memory loss. It's important to maintain aha's in consciousness; in other words, at the top of your thinking, by writing it down.

- Validate Your Multi-Dimensional Reality – Record what you uncover about "who is showing up" both at your trading desk and in other parts of your life; which personas come out during what issue, crisis or challenge.

- Access Unconscious Feelings – the act of writing can help access hidden information from deeper levels as the words flow out onto paper.

- Integrate Your Experiences – writing about your experiences can facilitate insight and deepen the level of assimilation so that information becomes a learned lesson.

The basic principle of EFT is: The underlying cause of all negative emotions is an imbalance in the body's energy system.

The theory states that negative emotions are built in the following stages:

1. A negative experience occurs;

2. Negative emotions are felt in response to this negative experience leading to inappropriate programming inside the body

3. The body's energy system gets disrupted due to these negative emotions

EFT teaches that, in order to remove the negative response, tackling the negative experience is not enough, because doing so cannot correct the energy imbalance. Rather, the energy imbalance must be restored along with curing the negative emotions.

The main difference between EFT an TFT lies not in principles, but in application. In TFT, a specific sequence of tapping points (know as a algorithm)

is used for a particular problem. This sequence is determined using a procedure borrowed from applied kinesiology or muscle testing. In EFT, the order and sequence of tapping points is deemed to be unimportant, and therefore there are no individual algorithms for different problems. Instead, a comprehensive algorithm is used for all problems, and no diagnosis or muscle testing is required.

Candace Pert, PhD author of *Molecules in Emotion*, is a researcher who has extensively documented the body/mind connection in healing both physical and emotional issues. Dr. Pert is best known for her opiate receptor, endorphin and peptide research. Her work is based on how the body/mind functions as a single psychosomatic network of information molecules, which control our health and physiology. She writes:

> "Quantum physics predicts that what we can visualize and observe becomes reality. It is insufficient to say mind and body are interconnected. Our "bodymind' "functions as a single psychosomatic network of information molecules. New paradigm technologies, such as imagery, energy psychology, and affirmations, use the fact that the bodymind is one dynamic field of energy and information to make healthful transformations. This field generates the molecules of emotion and cells of matter. Health comes from an Anglo-Saxon word for whole, related to the words wholesome and holy. A psychosomatic network generates cells, which secrete and respond to molecules throughout the bodymind."

Deepak Chopra, MD, an endocrinologist on the forefront of mind/body medicine, describes the process of neurotransmitter, or minute chemicals, that transmit impulses between the brain and the cells of the body in his book *Quantum Healing*:

> "Neurotransmitters are the runners that race to and fro from the brain telling every organ inside us of our emotions, desires, memories, intuitions, and dreams. None of these events are confined to the brain alone. Likewise, none of them are strictly mental, since they can be coded into chemical messages. Neurotransmitters touch the life of every cell. Wherever a thought wants to go, these chemicals must go too, and without them, no thoughts can exist. To think is to practice brain chemistry, promoting a cascade of responses throughout the body."

The discovery of neurotransmitters provides scientific proof that the body, emotions, and mind are all connected. Dr. Chopra says:

> "In my own practice, several cancer patients have recovered completely after being pronounced incurable and given only a few months to live. I didn't think they were miracles; I thought they were proof that the mind can go deep enough to change the very patterns that design the body. It can wipe mistakes off the blueprint, so to speak, and destroy any disease –cancer, diabetes, coronary heart disease – that has disturbed the design."

Negative thoughts and emotions have a physiological connection and have been shown to be extremely harmful. Positive thoughts and emotions have been shown to be extremely beneficial. EFT involves a powerful redirection of both the physiology of the brain/mind and energy flow of the body/mind to support the well-being and healing states necessary to create a tuned and formidable body/mind system as it was designed to be.

The EFT Technique in Action

EFT includes a series of processes. For the newcomer to meridian-based techniques, they may seem unusual, awkward, and even strange. The tapping to some may look silly, especially along with the chanting of affirmations out loud, but the results can be astounding and seem miraculous.

Each EFT technique serves a specific purpose. I will provide an overview of each here and, if you would like more information, a web link and as well book references will be provided. You will be asked to tap approximately seven times on each point, but you don't have to keep an exact count. Anywhere between five and ten is usually fine. Many get results even if they aren't tapping on the exact acupuncture points. However, points will be described as clearly as possible so that you can find them precisely. The EFT techniques work like a team and you may need to use more than one to achieve results. You may also have to repeat the procedure more than once to clear an emotional pattern completely. Using any technique or repetition of the process only takes a minute or two. With experience, you'll be able to release even complex emotional patterns in a relatively short period of time.

One last point has to do with the power of intent. Focusing your mind and intention on the issue at hand is very important. Being purposeful and intentional, not only about your tapping sequence and affirmation that encompasses the issue, but also to hold your attention to your intention during the entire process, is critical to getting the energy blockage clear. If you want to clear a fear of "pulling the trigger at the right time in a trade," but you are focused on a fun time you had while on your last vacation, you will affirm the good time on the vacation but the fear of pulling the trigger will remain. In order to help you maintain focus, a reminder phrase will be suggested for you to use at each tapping point. This phrase identifies the emotion you are clearing as you tap, and reminds the unconscious that you are working with a specific blockage.

Refer to page 237 for detailed information on performing the emotional field technique.

Self-Hypnosis

Hypnosis is an extremely powerful process for accessing the subconscious to influence a long list of behaviors, emotions, somatic complaints, beliefs and pain issues. Hypnosis is a particular form of trance or altered state of consciousness, relying on a specific set of instructions, which may or may not be provided in an induction. Hypnosis dates back to the 18th Century, when Franz Anton Mezmer induced a phenomenon he termed 'animal magnetism'. Soon the term 'mesmerism' was coined, where Mezmer would use suggestion to cure illnesses. Hypnosis did not come to be known by this name until Scottish physician James Braid used the Greek root for sleep, hypnos, to create the term. Hypnosis has been successfully used in surgery, dentistry, pain abatement, psychotherapy, weight loss, accelerated learning, and many other applications.

Hypnosis may be the quickest method known whereby someone, "an operator," somehow bypasses the conscious mind while initiating a sleeplike state to:

1) exploit the programmed paradigms of the subconscious mind

2) encode new desirable programs or erase old, undesirable ones through suggestion,

3) accelerate or ameliorate the natural mental process.

In other words, hypnosis is a choice technique for exploiting the subconscious, by circumventing the conscious mind. In hetero-hypnosis, the operator is another person. In self-hypnosis, the operator is your own conscious mind. However, hypnosis and self-hypnosis are virtually the same thing. If you have an "operator," then you have chosen and have given permission to yourself to listen to the suggestions of another and permission to yourself to follow them. Actually, it can be said that all hypnosis is self-hypnosis; the hypnotist is only a guide and a supporter of a process going on in the mind of the subject.

It is important to note that hypnosis, although associated quite often with sleep, is only a deeply relaxed state and not sleep-related. This state provides the internal environment for receptivity to suggestions. The trance state is not unconscious or unaware. It can be quite aware as an observer of what is in the surroundings and still be deeply in trance. Essentially, most people go into a state of trance or altered state of consciousness many times per day, and in fact there are those for whom "trance" state is their normal waking state. This is easily illustrated through the individual who, while trading, executes a series of disastrous decisions and later feels like it was a dream, wondering what happened.

To get a sense of what it feels like, it is helpful for the complete novice to go to a professional hypnotist at first. However, it is not absolutely necessary. You can record the suggestions given here in that you have a powerful voice and the process can work very well.

When beginning the process, it is best to be in a comfortable environment, free of distractions with soothing, quiet, and soft music to help the induction. With practice, your suggestions will become stronger and more effective. The induction can focus around something similar to "with every breath my focus is keen." Countdown from 10 to 0, then close your eyes.

Suggestions should be simple, short and totally positive. Also, moving toward what you want is more successful than moving away from that goal; i.e., "I follow my rules easily and effortlessly", not "I don't make mistakes or I don't have problems with following my rules". Leave a gap in the recording to add other suggestions about every 2 minutes is helpful and limit suggestions to 1 or 2 at a time, so as not to crowd the recording.

- Be clear in your speech: no uhms, ahhs or vague language.

- If your mind wanders, once you catch it, immediately go back to the suggestions.

- Form a clear mental image of each suggestion. The image should be sensory-rich in order to galvanize all the brain's centers.

  o See profitable entries and exits, see yourself with a very profitable portfolio, see yourself getting an award for a trading competition you won

  o The emphasis is on *you* in this process. It is not helpful to see other people thinking highly of you, or to make suggestions that focus on your image among others. The process is not about what people think about you.

The Attitude: The right motive is important. Know why you want what you want. This can't be emphasized enough. It is both unwise and unhealthy to desire dominance over others, or to want to sleep only four hours per night. In either case, the outcomes have consequences that outweigh any perceived benefit. The motive is best that has a deeper purpose, one that is positive, healthy, and community minded; for example, money for money's sake is a very poor reason to trade, but to support self and family and community gives a purpose with foundation, that is, one higher in aspiration and value.

It's best to have reasonable goals in addition to reasonable motives. Make your goals high, but not unrealistic. Self-hypnosis is not about wishing for miracles. Saying you'll make 100,000 million in the next week is more than unlikely, but having reachable goals for the week, month, year, 5-10 years can be done.

You must want and expect to attain the hypnotic state but must, above all, *let* yourself go into it. This intention around the state is a salient point. It is best to be relaxed and confident to achieve a state that is results- oriented. The keywords are "want" to be in the state of trance, "expect" to be in the state of trance and "let" the state of trance descend upon you.

The setting, especially in the first session is a noteworthy point. A warm comfortable room, free of drafts, with low light that is very, very quiet is conducive to a successful trance. If you are very uncomfortable, the critical internal censor will make it virtually impossible for you to be hypnotized, especially if cold. Also, a great aid would be to use earphones to quiet noise and focus attention.

Sit in a comfortable chair, lean back with headphones and listen to the recorded induction. If necessary, find a place void of distractions like an office after hours or some other place. With ample practice, you'll find you don't need the recording and the setting is unimportant. You'll find your own technique, for example 3 deep breaths and a count to 10, followed by relaxation coursing through your body, perhaps combined with an appropriate suggestion to induce whenever and wherever you want would be powerful; such as, before an important meeting, between greens in a golf game, as you begin to trade, or anytime.

Success will only come with constant practice. One session wonders can happen in horse shoes but is not probable in self-hypnosis; one session can take you from a B grade loser to an A grade loser. Integration of self-hypnosis into your routine of the day will make a successful formula. Listen to your recording twice per day, for best results. The more you practice forming a mental image of your recorded suggestions, the sooner you'll achieve your aims. A deep trance is not critical to success; the right suggestion pattern is what does it. Be cautious about trying too hard—"the harder you try the harder it becomes". Tension happens, both psychic and physical. The internal critic says, "See? You can't do it." If this happens immediately go back to suggestions for relaxing and breathing. You can't force your mind to accept suggestion; it will be engaged and gently invited to make progress. You must adopt a detached attitude, wanting, expecting, and then letting. Finally, the fear of letting go haunts some folks. This is a helpful suggestion: "You are safe and secure. If the doorbell rings or someone happens to come in, you will open your eyes, arise, and feel totally refreshed, totally alert and capable of handling any situation. To awaken from the state all you have to do is say, "I will wake up on the count of three, 1, 2, 3, and you will be wide awake and back to normal."

All throughout this book we have talked about the mental domain or our thoughts and the notion that our thoughts—conscious or unconscious—are driven by our MAPs. We have discussed the power of emotion as in anxiety, fear, greed and euphoria, and how it can distort our thoughts and lead to the physical manifestation of behaviors like impulsivity and compulsivity. These three domains are also the portals that, if accessed, can lead to effective reprogramming through self-hypnosis. The self hypnosis exercise is designed to identify 3 "keys" to open and access the physical, emotional and mental domains in order to reprogram the MAPs, mental models and paradigms of the subconscious causing misperception and distortion and to support those strengths. For instructions on the self hypnosis exercise, refer to page 229.

Meditation

Due to the analysis necessary and the focus warranted in the process of trading, distraction, whether from external or internal sources, can disrupt your effectiveness severely. Consequently, there is great value in being aligned, centered and grounded in order to optimize all of the system's resources toward seeing reality for what it is, being on the right side of the order flow, and dancing with the price action by following its lead. Among the many ways that address alignment, centeredness and groundedness, few are as powerful as meditation. Over the years, the efficacy of meditation has been scientifically documented with regard to physiological, mental, emotional and behavioral benefits. Some of those benefits include:

- Sharpening attention

- Lowering heart rate

- Lowering stress levels

- Easing anxiety

- Increasing patience

- Inducing calm

- Reducing susceptibility to fear and greed

With consistency, this powerful exercise supports the entire system of mind/body and spirit.

It is generally held that meditation has an Eastern derivation, and the earliest can be said to be religious in philosophy. All the major religions harbor their own form of meditation to include, to name a few:

- Bahai Faith

- Buddhism

- Christianity

- Hinduism

- Islam

- Jainism

- Judaism

- Sikhism

- Taoism

New Age and other secular forms can be added to the list as well. Covering all corners of the planet, even though there are myriad forms with differing structures, there is a common theme of calming, centering, aligning and grounding the mind/body. Meditation is a journey with no destination, a journey that enters into the depths of heart and soul to open the self to a deeper conversation with the higher centers of being.

One of the tenants of meditation is the concept of being fully present and in the moment. Being fully present means the mind/body system is living and vibrating in this moment, undeterred by distractions emanating from the internal or external. Being fully present means the focus is on the task at hand while remaining on purpose, on target. So often, while trading or being involved in some other endeavor, we are thinking about what happened in the last trade, the last hour, yesterday or what is coming up in the next few moments or tomorrow. In other words, we are everywhere but where we should be, focused on what is taking place right now. Distractions can come in the form of errant emotions like fear, greed, anxiety and euphoria, all of which can distort perception to wild degrees, making the non-existent seem real. Consistent meditation hones an appreciation for just "being," without timetables, goals, effort or hubris. Trying harder yields diminishing returns while surrender and letting things be are prescriptions for success (success being defined as sitting, standing or walking in the quiet serenity of the self and allowing the march of things either in our head or in the "hood" to go on while we are in it, but not of it). For instructions on the meditation exercise, refer to page 226.

Appendix

Exercise: Meditation

The meditation exercise I am going to share with you is akin to a "Mindful Meditation" John Kabot Zinn talks about in his book, *Full Catastrophe Living*. The great thing about meditation is that doing it only requires doing nothing.

Sit down in a chair, or on a pillow, or on the floor. The point is to get comfortable. You'll want to keep your back straight in order to facilitate the energy flow up and down your spine. If you sit in a chair, put your feet flat on the floor, maintaining the energy flow in a constant and facilitated state. The eastern philosophies of China, India and the like speak of the energies Chi and Prana. Chi is the Chinese word used to describe "the natural energy of the Universe." This energy, though called "natural," is spiritual or supernatural, and is part of a metaphysical, not an empirical, belief system. Chi is thought to permeate all things, including the human body. Prana is a Sanskrit word meaning 'breath' and refers to a vital, life-sustaining force of living beings and vital energy. Prana is a central concept in Indian medicine and Yoga, where it is believed to flow through a network of fine subtle channels, but principally through the nostrils.

Now, take your attention and focus it on an external or internal point such as an imaginary candlelight or picturing your navel. The point is not to try to concentrate energy—that would be an act of doing—but to focus the attention and let the mind be free of thinking. Allow the thoughts to come and go with an intention of un-attachment to any thought. The breath is especially helpful by deeply inhaling through the nose and slowly exhaling through the mouth with the lips pursed as if blowing out a candle. This could be done to a cadence count of

4 – 6 – or 8, pausing after each inhale with the same count, then slowly exhaling to that same count. The breath is very important, as it is a cleansing action and oxygenates the blood stream while helping to dilate blood vessels and send more oxygen to the brain, which has a calming effect on the entire body. A mantra might also be used; it is a religious or mystical phrase of one or more syllables, typically from the Sanskrit language. Their use varies according to the school and philosophy associated with the mantra. Mantras are mostly accepted as having a religious derivation in the Vedic religion of India; but their use has morphed over the centuries to support the single-minded focus of the meditation process. Chanting a brief phrase or mantra, either out loud or silently, helps to focus the attention and let go of thought. It is important to be attuned to the process not as "trying" but "being" in order to allow the mind/body to resonate with the stillness and quiet. It is said that for every hour of meditation, the body gets the equivalent of 4 hours of rest.

As you breath deeply and evenly to the cadence of the count, let go of any thought, care or issue and, when it returns, acknowledge it and allow it to be there without judgment. This may be difficult at first, but just keep the intention strong and, with time, you will be able to sit in quiet stillness with only the sound of either your breathing or the chant of the mantra as your thoughts to come and go. Eventually your ability to just "be" will become stronger and you may find you are held captive less and less by unruly thoughts.

'Om' or 'aum' is a universal mantra that works well for assisting in letting go of thoughts. It's derivation is Chinese and it is a mystical or sacred syllable in the Dharmic religions. It is placed at the beginning of most Hindu texts as a sacred exclamation to be uttered at the beginning and end of a reading of any prayer or mantra. Chant or say the word silently, repeatedly, along with the cadence of your breathing. Let me emphasize that the mantra is not necessary, but may be of help. It is perfectly OK and, in fact, preferable by many to just sit and focus your attention on your breathing. This is a very powerful way to proceed.

It is advisable to practice meditation at the same time everyday to help instill the habit and routine, especially when beginning. It's a perfect way to start your day before you do anything else. It can rejuvenate, align, invigorate and charge your system, infusing you with an sharpened sense of attention to what matters. It's also a wonderful way to end the day to wind down, de-stress, realign, shed tension, calm the system, and generally defuse any negative energy that could disrupt a good night's sleep. A mediation break at lunch is an excellent tool to maintain balance and focus for the day to weed out distractions and remain on purpose and on task. As you can see, any time might be the best time for you. You choose. Additionally, you may want to develop a two-a-day practice, once in the morning and once in the evening, as a powerful way to instill and maintain a sense of calm intention throughout the day and night.

There is no set time interval to meditate but, generally speaking, 20 to 30 minutes is what many employ. John Kabat-Zinn speaks of 45 minutes for those who use the mindful meditative process. For beginners, I usually suggest that they start with 5 minutes and work their way into longer time frames until they are able to remain still and focused for 20 to 45 minutes. A small and non-intrusive timer might be used in the beginning to support your practice.

Commonly reported results from meditation include:

- Greater religious or spiritual faith

- An increase in patience, compassion

- Deep relaxation and feelings of calm, peace and/or profound moments of joy

- Heightened sensitivity to environmental irritants like fluorescent lighting

- Heightened sense perception

- Increase of focus and intentional intensity

- Increased ability to sustain and maintain commitments

- Increased centeredness and groundedness

What is provided here is but a brief introduction to the basics of meditation, and I would encourage you to get started, but to also do more research on your own and perhaps enlist the help of a teacher in the form you most resonate with. You might begin with your religious/spiritual advisor or with a yoga teacher. The deeper you'd like to go, the more helpful it is to have a guide.

Exercise: Self Hypnosis

Let's begin. You may need to record these instructions to follow them. Once you have identified the "keys" to your subconscious mind, you will use the same self-induction process to embed suggestions. Find a comfortable position and take at least 3 very deep breaths while holding each as long as you can and then exhaling very slowly through your mouth, as if blowing out a candle. Now, focus on your breathing, in and out, and begin to let go of any thoughts, cares and concerns, giving yourself permission to let go and feel relaxed. Now take your attention into your feet and give your feet permission to feel relaxed and calm while visualizing or imagining in your minds eye that a mist is beginning to gather around your feet. Tell yourself that this fog or mist is very pleasurable and that your feet are beginning to feel better and better. Notice that the fog is rising up around your ankles and calves, and as it rises, tell yourself that your legs are allowed to relax and enjoy the pleasurable feeling from the fog. Give your body permission to relax, slow down and enjoy this experience. Then notice that the fog is traveling up over your thighs, hips and buttocks while giving your thighs, hips, and buttocks permission to feel relaxed and calm. As the fog travels up, it surrounds your stomach, heart-space, hands, forearms and shoulder areas while you tell yourself it is OK to be relaxed and feel good, giving your stomach, heart-space, hands, forearms and shoulder areas permission to relax. Now, notice the fog is engulfing your neck and head as you give your neck and head muscles permission to let go of any tension, stress, and concerns in order to relax and feel good.

Now, I am going to offer you 3 keys to unlock the physical, emotional and mental portals of your being. In doing so, I will suggest to you a series of words in three stages. Each stage will correspond to a key. You will be asked to visualize or imagine each word to whatever degree or intensity level that surfaces for you by repeating the word to yourself. When you have repeated each word separately and have visualized or imagined to whatever degree you will pass that thought and will be given another word. After all of the words have been experienced to whatever degree in that particular stage, you will then choose the word you felt or experienced to the greatest degree and that will be your key for that stage.

Now that you are relaxed and focused, we will begin. The first key will be your physical key. Take your attention into your extremities, hands, feet, and/or face.

I will give you a list of words, one at a time, and ask you to repeat that word to yourself while visualizing or imagining the experience of that word in the extremities of your body. You will file away in the back of your mind the level of the experience and later when we have finished with this list you will choose the word you felt to the greatest degree and that will be your physical key, designed to give easy and effortless access to the physical domain of your body. When you have chosen this word, it is only for you to know and use, as it is a powerful way to begin to gain access to your inner world.

The first word is heavy. Heavy. Visualize or imagine the word heavy in your mind to whatever degree of intensity you are able, while repeating the word to yourself over and over again. Heavy. Heavy. Now pass that thought and file the intensity of the experience away in the back of your mind to be retrieved later in this session.

The next word is light. Light. Visualize or imagine the word light in your mind to whatever degree of intensity you are able, while repeating the word to yourself over and over again. Light. Light. Now pass that thought and file the intensity of the experience away in the back of your mind to be retrieved later in this session.

The next word is tingling. Tingling. Visualize or imagine the word tingling in your mind to whatever degree of intensity you are able, while repeating the word to yourself over and over again. Tingling. Tingling. Experience tingling in your extremities to whatever degree. Now pass that thought and file the intensity of the experience away in the back of your mind to be retrieved later in this session.

The next word is warm. Warm. Visualize or imagine the word warm in your mind to whatever degree of intensity you are able, while repeating the word warm to yourself over and over again. Warm. Warm. Experience warm in your body to whatever degree. Now pass that thought and file the intensity of the experience away in the back of your mind to be retrieved later in this session.

Now, I'd like for you to revisit and recall each word and the corresponding experience and choose which word you experienced to the greatest degree. When you have chosen the word or experience you felt to the greatest degree, that will be your physical key. This is your key and is only meant for you. We will allow a few moments for you to do this and afterward we will move on to the next stage and identify your emotional key.

The next domain or key will be your emotional key. Take your attention into your chest or heart space. I will give you a list of words, one at a time, and ask you to repeat that word to yourself while visualizing or imagining the experience of that word emotionally. After you have experienced this word emotionally to whatever degree you will file away in the back of your mind the level of the experience and later when we have finished with this list you will choose the word you emotionally felt to the greatest degree and that will be your emotional key, designed to give easy and effortless access to the your emotional domain. When you have chosen this word, it is only for you to know and use, as it is a powerful way to begin to gain access to your inner world.

The first word is calm. Calm. Visualize or imagine feeling the word calm in your mind and heart space to whatever degree of intensity you are able, while repeating the word to yourself over and over again. Calm. Calm. Experience what it emotionally feels like to be calm. Now pass that thought and file the intensity of the experience away in the back of your mind to be retrieved later in this session.

The next word is excitement. Excitement. Visualize or imagine feeling the word excitement in your mind and heart space to whatever degree of intensity you are able, while repeating the word to yourself over and over again. Excitement. Excitement. Experience what it emotionally feels like to be in excitement. Now pass that thought and file the intensity of the experience away in the back of your mind to be retrieved later in this session.

The next word is safe. Visualize or imagine feeling the word safe in your mind and heart space to whatever degree of intensity you are able, while repeating the word to yourself over and over again. Safe. Safe. Experience what it emotionally feels like to be safe. Now pass that thought and file the intensity of the experience away in the back of your mind to be retrieved later in this session.

The last word is love. Visualize or imagine feeling the word love in your mind and heart space to whatever degree of intensity you are able, while repeating the word to yourself over and over again. Love. Love. Experience what it emotionally feels like to be in love. Now pass that thought and file the intensity of the experience away in the back of your mind to be retrieved later in this session.

Now, I'd like for you to revisit and recall each word and the corresponding emotional experience and choose which word you experienced to the greatest degree. When you have chosen the word or experience you felt to the greatest degree, that will be your emotional key. This is your key and is only meant for you. We will allow a few moments for you to do this and afterward we will move on to the next stage and identify your mental key.

The next domain or key will be your mental key. Take your attention into your forehead in the space between your eyes, or otherwise known in some esoteric eastern philosophies as your third eye. I will count from 5 to 0 as you count along with me. There is only one word phrase for this domain, and it is deep sleep. Repeat the words deep sleep out loud and if your eyes are not closed already then close them when you have reached 0. All right, ready, 5 – 4 – 3 – 2 – 1 – 0 deep sleep. Deep sleep.

And now, letting go of all cares, tensions, worries, troubles and concerns allow yourself to sink even deeper into your body. You may begin to notice your breath is deep and easy or you may notice your body is even more relaxed and peaceful. With every breath, you may find you are going deeper and deeper into a state of relaxation and peace or you may find you are more comfortable than you have been in a long time.

Now, I would like for you to visualize or imagine a vehicle. It is among your most favorite ways of traveling and may be a train, or a plane, or a boat or a beautiful car. Take a moment to notice your vehicle is now waiting for you to board it. PAUSE HERE   Now that you are aboard and in your vehicle, take a moment to decide where you'd like to go. It will, upon your command, take you easily and effortlessly to your favorite environment of all, whether it is inside or outside, in a lavish mansion or on a wide, sandy secluded beach or on another planet in the Universe. I'm going to pause for a few moments for you to take a pleasurable ride to that destination. PAUSE HERE.

It is a beautiful place with just the right amount of light and the perfect temperature. Look around and notice what you see. The colors may be brilliant or full and vibrant; the smells are inviting with scents that lift you up, there may be music serenading you as well, just the right kind of music you can change or modify to your exact specifications. Recognize and realize this is your space, in fact it is your power place, your play space, your workspace for constructing the most creative and best ways to solve any problem, or concern you may bring. And, now you may notice whatever you desire as a tool, accommodation, apparatus, device, gadget, machine or equipment it is at your disposal. All you need to do is create it in your space. It might be a powerful computer or a telephone to call upon anyone in the universe to consult with your challenge or concern. And, you can change or modify these devices whenever and however you choose. Next, you can furnish this space with anything you desire for comfort and/or efficiency: lounge chairs, overstuffed couches, marble desks, or nothing at all. It is all up to you and in accordance with your slightest whim. This is your power place, your sanctuary where no one can intrude, take it away, or hurt you. It is your play space, your work place, and your thought oasis. All yours and for all time.

Now, recognize and realize you may feel rejuvenated, revitalized and renewed just by being in your private power space, allowing every organ, physical system, muscle, fiber and nerve to heal and respond to this healing energy space with vitality and strength. You may be feeling fantastic or you may be feeling intentional and connected with your strengths and focus. Know that you can return at any time and feel exactly the same or better each and ever time you access this space. Every atom, molecule and cell in your body is responding with joy and well being, ready to do your bidding.

In a moment, I'm going to count from 0 to 5 and when I reach 5 you will be wide-awake, feeling refreshed, energized and focused. 0 you are beginning to climb back into your vehicle for a brief trip back to now; 1 your system is slowly and easily waking and coming back into the room; 2 you may notice feeling in places previously out of your awareness or you may feel your body responding to waking; 3 you may notice you are feeling focused, refreshed and energized, ready to take on your next task easily and effortlessly; 5 wide awake, wide awake.

With practice, this will be a powerful tool for addressing any issue, challenge or problem you face. You may want to develop a list of "projects" or issues you'd like to work on. Work on no more than 3 at a time and remember to visualize and imagine yourself (as yourself) successfully achieving whatever it is that you desire. The bottom line is that, for it to work, you've got to use it.

Exercise: Emotional Field Technique

There are two tapping sequences. The first sequence is a starting point for all EFT clearing. It takes about a minute or so to perform the short sequence once you have identified the issue you want to address. Phillip and Jane Mountrose in their book, *Getting Thru,* have a particularly concise explanation.

1) *The Setup.* First identify an issue and be as specific as you can. The process works best when we are intentional and have a specific emotion to clear. For instance, anxiety or fear is better than "an inability to pull the trigger on a trade." Similarly, if you are experiencing a physical challenge or a pain, it is important to be specific with that as well by identifying not only the specific area or pain but also the emotion associated with it; for example, having a backache and identifying "worry and stress" as the associated emotion. Focus on bringing an emotion or issue into your awareness in the present moment. The key to the success of the process is to feel the emotion and set up the disruption in the meridian system.

2) *The Evaluation.* When you have brought the emotion up to its full intensity (or whatever intensity feels comfortable), measure how strong it feels between 1 and 10. This involves using a subjective unit of distress (SUD), 1 being least and 10 being the most you are experiencing. The goal is to eliminate the negative emotional content or bring it to zero. It is important to identify how you feel about it "now" and evaluate this level, not the starting level. If you can't put a number on it, just take note of how you feel now (before) the tapping, and after, take note again.

3) *The Affirmation.* Unconscious blockages can occur as a result of events that go back to early childhood and may prevent you from achieving results with EFT. This phenomenon is known as Psychological Reversal (PR). Gary Craig compares it to having a battery in backwards. Your portable radio may have enough power, but it will never play music. Something is unconsciously preventing you from succeeding. This is

addressed through the repetition of an affirmation that releases judgments and limiting beliefs. Craig and Fowlie estimate psychological reversal is only present about 40 percent of the time.

4) *The Tapping Sequence.* Begin the tapping sequence immediately after completing the affirmation. As you tap on each point, repeat a reminder phrase (just one or two words) one time aloud. It helps you to stay focused on the issue. The tapping points are acupuncture points, so they are generally tender to the touch.

5) The Re-Evaluation. When you have completed the tapping sequence, take a moment to focus on the emotion or issue again and notice how it feels. Evaluate it again between one and ten to bring any difference in your experience into your awareness.

Other areas:

- The eyebrow: This point is at the inside edge of the eyebrow, above the inside corner of the eye

- Side of the Eye: This point is next to the outside of the eye, on the middle of the temple.

- Under the Eye: This point is just below the middle of the eye, near the edge of the bone.

- Under the Nose: This point is in the indentation just between the middle of the nose and the middle of the upper lip.

- Chin: This point is on the middle of the chin, just below the crease.

- Collarbone: This point is one of the trickier ones to locate. It is a tender area close to the end of the collarbone, next to the u-shaped indentation below the neck, just under the bone.

- Under the Arm: This point is in the tender area on the side of the chest, about four inches below the armpit

Of course, one time through on the short sequence will seldom neutralize a substantive emotional or physiological issue. You may need to not only repeat the process, but initiate the Long Sequence. But before that, consider the following points if the issue or emotion remains. Philip and Jane Mountrose provide the following instructions.

- *Partial Relief:* The intensity of the emotion is lower than when you started, but it is still above a two in intensity. This means there is another aspect of the emotion or issue to examine. The next step is to repeat the Short Sequence to clear the remaining emotion.

- *Nearly Complete Relief:* The intensity of the emotion is down to two or less, so there is just as small residue left. In most cases, this residue will release with a short process called the Floor-to-Ceiling Eye Roll. Try this one next. If the emotion clears, you are done. If not, repeat the Short Sequence.

- *Complete Relief:* The intensity is gone completely. In this case, focus on being in a situation you are likely to experience in the future that would previously have triggered the emotion or issue. Imagine yourself there to see if you get any emotional intensity. If you do, you can repeat the Short Sequence to clear the remaining intensity. If you cannot come up with any intensity, the pattern may be completely gone.

- *Little or No Relief:* The emotional intensity has not changed or you have completed several rounds and the intensity has not changed much. When this happens, we recommend using the Complete Sequence, which is described later.

If you do not notice any difference in the quality of the emotion other than intensity, you can repeat the procedure with the same emotion. In this case, you need to distinguish it from the disruption you cleared in the first round by calling it something slightly different like, "This remaining _____." If you said, "This fear" the first time, call it "This remaining fear" the second time.

The Floor-to-Ceiling Eye Roll. This short but effective process takes only a few moments to complete. Use it whenever you have reduced the intensity of an issue to two or less with the Short or Complete Sequence but haven't reached zero. The tapping is recommended to be performed twice with the "Nine Gamut Process" sandwiched in.

1) The Evaluation: Normally this process would be used if the Short Sequence and/or the Complete Sequence has reduced the SUD level to 1 or 2.

2) The Tapping Sequence: Begin by looking straight ahead and tapping continuously on the Gamut Spot. This spot is located on the back of your hand exactly between the knuckle of your little finger and the knuckle of your ring finger. Hold your head still while shifting only your eyes to look as far down towards the floor as possible. While focusing on the issue and continuing to tap on the Gamut Point,

gradually move your gaze slowly up toward the ceiling (taking about 6 seconds to do this) until you are looking up as far as you can while not moving your head. Repeat once the reminder phrase you have chosen for this emotion, "This _____."

3) The Re-evaluation: When finished, revisit the emotion and take stock of the intensity as before from 1 to 10. In most cases this should be 0, but if not, you may want to continue with the Short Sequence or the Complete Sequence.

Exercise: Identify Your Macro and Micro Purpose
This exercise is designed to help you conduct an internal search through imagery and specific questions to support your identification of a macro and micro purpose.

THE EULOGY: One Hundred Years From Now.
Often individuals desire the answers to why they cannot break bad habits or include new empowering behaviors in their repertoire, but they do not know the right question to ask. This exercise is designed to free your (right brain) unconscious process by asking the right questions in a context that causes inner curiosity—an automatic search.

Use a separate sheet of paper to make notes of what your eulogy read.

Example: Jonathan Dousman was a good provider for his family and always was there when he was needed. He was both loved and respected. He was lovable, fun to be around and hard working. He was also a leader in his family as well as in business with his keen ability to listen and be supportive without telling people how to run their lives. He was also financially successful but used his money and his time to help others that were less fortunate than himself. He was active in his community and prepared to give of himself in order so that the good of the whole would be realized. He will be greatly missed leaving a legacy of integrity, honesty, achievement and investment of self to his family and friends.

Limitless Wishing

Many people are plagued by their own limited thinking, which serves as a psychological strait jacket that constricts creativity and the possibilities desired. This exercise positively addresses limited thinking by giving you permission to think BIG. In this opportunity, you can have ANYTHING in the world with these conditions:

It be humanly possible to give

It must be specific (example: money is only a medium to get what you want; you cannot consume money in any way).

After you have allowed yourself to venture on the journey, write your 3 wishes here:

1.

2.

3.

Limitless Thinking

You have identified 3 of your greatest wishes and you have been asked to imagine your life after receiving the first one. As you are thinking about how your life would be different, allow all of your senses to explore the taste, smell, sound, feel, and look of those differences. Really let your imagination go and notice the smallest of details; for instance, clothing style and color, home, friends, physical body, job performance and automobile to name a number of them. After you have finished, note all of the changes you have identified below.

Encyclopedia of Biographies

About 250 years from now, an encyclopedia has stories of the lives of prominent people who lived a long time ago. Among these biographies is the brief life story of you. Sit back and relax, while allowing your mind to take you into the future and read about all you accomplished in your lifetime. Take as much time as you like. The example may help you to do this exercise so you may want to read it before you "read" your biography.

After listening to the instructor's guided journey, take about 5 minutes to "read" your biography. As before, let your imagination and inner voice lead you in this exercise. Remember "the book" has information from your childhood to your senior years of life. It has chronicled your greatest achievements, accomplishments, and contributions to society and any other significant events of your life. As before, when you have finished, write your "biography" below.

Example: Although Jane Doesman did not graduate from college until later in life, she was a paragon of inspiration to other women and men. In her early years, she worked as a secretary before her 21st birthday. As she exhibited a work ethic and ability to remain focused, she worked her way up into the management ranks. First she became an account executive, soon leading the division, and then the nation, in sales. While she sold, she took many business seminars, training courses and management workshops along the way, putting her newfound tools to great use as she continued to increase her production. As time went on, she used her knowledge to create new procedures and methods that increased the company's overall effectiveness and market share.

When she became a manager, she was often described as a stern taskmaster who was demanding and maintained a high degree of excellence; however, she was always respected by those who disagreed with her, as well as her friends. She was fair, compassionate and sensitive as much as she was a hard driver.

By the time she left the company, she had become one of the most revered, powerful and creative leaders the company had ever enjoyed, leaving behind a legacy of innovative management techniques that have been adopted by the business community at large.

ENCYCLOPEDIA OF BIOGRAPHIES: Additional work page:

Take One Minute

You have only 1 year to live. What are you going to do with the time left?

Write Your Own Macro Purpose

After writing your purpose: Look at it as if you were your best friend, and write 3 trading pursuits you should be involved in.

Exercise: The Power Circle

The following is an extremely effective exercise based upon the neuro-linguistic programming techniques of anchoring and pattern interrupts. It is called "Power Circle." It is so named because it can literally shift your focus and galvanize your intention for getting the results you want in a matter of seconds. This would be an important weapon in your power arsenal you can employ in the heat of market battle when you become aware you are held hostage by delinquent internal patterns that, if unchecked, will quickly erode your portfolio. This is an effective and fast-working technique for activating strong and empowering emotions associated with the wins of your past.

First, stand with enough room around you to envision or imagine a circle in front of you. It should be about 2 to 3 feet in diameter or enough room that you can comfortably step into it from where you are standing. Next, visualize or imagine your favorite color and color the circle as though you painted it, or as if there were a colored spotlight shining into and coloring the circle. Now, take 2 to 3 deep breaths and allow your body to relax. If you like, you may close your eyes; it may intensify the experience for you. Next, you will remember a time either long ago or in your recent past an event seminal to your life. It represents you at your best and at a time you felt aligned, connected, powerful and successful, at a time where everything seemed to be and go just right. As you visualize and imagine this experience, notice your environment. Are you in or outdoors? If outdoors, notice the lighting: sunny and bright, or overcast? Notice the richness of your surroundings. Are you in a meadow with grass and trees, or a walkway in front of an important building? Whichever is significant for you, see it as detailed and as clearly as possible. Notice the temperature and feel it. Associate into the experience as if you were there right now feeling things in your body. If indoors, notice the same detail, colors, significant items, room temperature, smells, sounds, and tastes. Also notice what you are wearing—the color and type of outfit. Look down at your shoes. What type are they and what do they look like? Colors, textures, etc. Fill your senses completely with your recollection of the event as possible. Now, begin to notice how you feel—strong, euphoric, loving, excited, etc. And, notice if there are others and what they are doing, saying, singing, etc.

Now, we will anchor the experience so that you can activate it whenever you like to use these emotions of empowerment as a resource in situations that warrant it. When you have felt the emotions and feel yourself fully associated into the experience, take your dominant hand and rub the back of your neck or your thigh or other body part. When you have felt this experience to its greatest degree, release the squeeze and allow the afterglow to resonate over your body. Repeat this process several times in order to strengthen the access. With practice, you will be able to retrieve the full experience of that event and use it as a powerful resource. The great thing is that it will only take you literally seconds to go through the entire technique. After you have done this once, and every time that you initiate the technique, be sure to step out of the circle.

Exercise: Stop Challenge & Choose

This is another pattern-interrupt exercise. It is a tool for getting different and more desired results, especially in your relationships. It can be used whenever one feels other than positive or neutral. In other words, positive feelings lead to positive behaviors that lead to positive results. Neutral feelings mean there is no real investment in the outcome and the results usually reflect the neutral nature of the emotions. Other than positive or neutral feelings, which are often described as negative, are reactionary, uncomfortable, disturbing and can be extremely distracting; for example, anger, fear, hatred, jealousy, envy, greed, frustration, anxiety, sadness, and grief are a few. Stop, Challenge and Choose is designed to aid in producing more of the long-term desired results we'd like to have in our lives.

We are driven by automatic responses. They are default positions triggered in certain situations. There are certain people, places and events that elicit specific responses (reactions) from you. It may seem you have no control over these events and they "just happen." It's like a pre-written script, and you are acting out your part, whether you want to or not. Automatic reactions for the most part don't produce long-term, desired results, i.e., healthy relationships, or winning positions; they garner temporary relief from uncomfortable feelings. The results they produce are usually short-term and designed to lessen the intensity of emotion we are feeling.

Examples of temporary relief would be:

- Yelling

- Procrastinating

- Eating

- Withdrawing

- Ignoring

- Blaming

- Minimizing

- Drinking Alcohol

- Avoiding

To catch ourselves BEFORE we respond automatically, we must use a process like SCC.

The process of SCC is:

1) When we become aware of an emotion that is other than positive or neutral, stop and do not react or respond. Examples of feelings other than positive or neutral:

- Anxious

- Apathetic

- Confused

- Frustrated

- Irritated

- Frightened

- Angry

When we notice these emotions, stop, take a deep breath and don't respond.

---

2) Challenge our thinking (since it's usually a perception of the event that causes the emotional response).

3) Consciously choose a response most likely to produce our long-term desired result.

STOP. Whenever you become aware that you feel less than positive or neutral. Retraining our brains. In the results model, instead of reacting to the interpretation or to what we made up in an unconscious manner. To intervene in our thinking. To breath deeply, count to 10, lower shoulders, don't respond. Center—physiology. Check your posture—are you coiling, ready to strike? Unclench anything that is. Begin to assume a posture of personal control. Stand straight, knees slightly bent, and put your focus on your center of gravity.

CHALLENGE. Ask yourself the following questions: What must I be telling myself, or believing that has resulted in my feeling this way? Is there another possible interpretation? What is the objective data? Look for the evidence of what is objectively true rather than what you are making up.

CHOOSE. Choose a response most likely to be your optimal response so that it most lines up with objective reality and is most likely to produce your long-term desired result.

An awareness of the feelings is important. Learn to identify feelings as they are occurring. Being able to notice and identify feelings in the moment allows us to stop and not respond in an automatic way. Once we've stopped, we can take a deep breath and assess whether or not our thinking lines up with objective reality. Most often, we will discover our feelings are based on something we "made up" about the other person and their intentions. If we are able to honestly challenge our thinking and not the other person, we will gain enough perspective to choose an emotionally mature response that represents the kind of person we would most like to be.

When first practicing this tool, you may notice only after the fact that you could have responded differently. This is a natural part of the process. Awareness is key and must be built before you can begin to direct your behavior differently. Soon you'll start to notice your automatic response; it will no longer be acceptable to you and you'll be willing to take the risk to behave differently. You'll be willing to look awkward and be uncomfortable in order to reach a bigger goal (namely, that of responding more in line with how you'd like to be). It gets better with practice. Fake it till you make it (even if it feels phony at first).

2-Minute Emergency Room Drill

Emergency medical personnel have a common practice—a process—they use every time they encounter a medical emergency. It's called the ABC's.

They ask three questions:

1) Do they have an airway?

2) Are they breathing?

3) Is there circulation?

53rd patient:

1) Do they have an airway?

---

2) Are they breathing?

3) Is there circulation?

900th patient:

1) Do they have an airway?

2) Are they breathing?

3) Is there circulation?

The point is, different emergencies—same process. As in an emergency room triage, you've got to step back and determine what is most important in producing the results you want for your trading and your life (what is in the best interest of your highest self)? The drill of SCC will help you stay calm and engage the emotions most appropriate to the situation and to solving the specific problem that the trade or the situation presents.

Bibliography

Bandler, R., Grinder, J. *Frogs into Princes: Neuro Linguistic Programming*. Moab, UT: Real People Press., (1979). 149(pp.15,24,30,45,52).

Bandler, Richard & John Grinder. *The Structure of Magic I: A Book About Language and Therapy*. Palo Alto, CA: Science & Behavior Books. (1975).

Benson, Herbert, MD. *The Relaxation Response* - (25th Anniversary Edition), Harper Collins, (2000).

Bogen, Joseph and Glenda, De Zure, R., Tenhouten, W.D. *The Other Side Of The Brain*: The A/P Ratio. Bull. L. A. Neurol. Soc. 37:39-61, 1972.

Carrol, John B. (ed.). *Language, Thought, and Reality: Selected Writings of Benjamin Lee Whorf*. Cambridge, Mass.: Technology Press of Massachusetts Institute of Technology 1956, 1997.

Callahan, Ph.D, Roger J. *Five Minute Phobia Cure: Dr. Callahan's Treatment for Fears, Phobias and Self-Sabotage*, NTC Publishing Group, 2000.

Clemens, Pierre. *Power Hypnosis: A Guide for Faster Learning and Greater Self-Mastery* (1979).

Chopra, Deepak, MD. *Quantum Healing,* Bantum Books (1990).

Cunningham, Les, PhD. *HypnoSport: The Creative Use of Hypnosis to Maximize Athletic Performance*; Westwood Publishing, Glendale, CA (1981).

Davidson, Richard PhD, Vilas Professor of Psychology and Psychiatry

Gallup, G.G. Jr. Chimpanzees: Self Recognition. *Science*, 167, 86-87. (1970).

Goleman, D. *Emotional Intelligence*. New York: Bantam Books. (1995).

Erickson, Milton H., Ernest L. Rossi. *Hypnotic Realities* , Halsted Press (January 1976).

Erickson, Milton H., Ernest L. Rossi. *Hypnotherapy - An Exploratory Casebook* John Wiley & Sons Inc; 1st edition (October 1979).

Erickson, Milton H., Ernest L. Rossi. *Experiencing Hypnosis* Irvington Publishers; Har/Cas edition (August 1981).

Helmstetter, Shad Ph.D. *The Self-Talk Solution*, Pocket Books, 1988.

Horowitz, Mardi. *Cognitive Psychodynamics From Conflict To Character*, John Wiley & Sons, Inc. New York.

Jung, C. G.; Adler, G. and Hull, R. F. C., eds. *Collected Works of C. G. Jung, Volume 18: The Symbolic Life: Miscellaneous Writings,* Princeton, NJ: Princeton University Press. (1977).

Kabat-Zinn J., Lipworth L, Burney R. *The clinical use of mindfulness meditation for the self-regulation of chronic pain.* Journ. Behav. Medicine. Jun;8(2):163-90. PubMed abstract PMID 3897551. (1985).

Kabat-Zinn, Jon. *Full Catastrophy Living:Using the Wisdom of Your Body and Mind to Face Stres, Pain, and Illness, (*1990) Dell Publishing .

Knight, Sue. *NLP at Work: Neurolingustic Programming, The Difference that makes a Difference.* London: Nicholas Brealey Publishing., 373. (1999).

Kunkel, Fritz, *Selected Writings* (Paperback) Publisher: Paulist Pr; Revised ed. edition (January 1984).

Rosenthal, R. *Pygmalion Effects: Existence, Magnitude, and Social Importance.* EDUCATIONAL RESEARCHER 16 (1987): 37-40. , and Jacobson, L. PYGMALION IN THE CLASSROOM: TEACHER EXPECTATION AND PUPILS' INTELLECTUAL DEVELOPMENT. New York: Holt, Rinehart and Winston, Inc., 1968.

Rossi, Ernest L. *The Psychobiology of Mind-Body Healing: New Concepts of Therapeutic Hypnosis.* New York, NY: W. W. Norton & Company, Inc., (1993).

Meichenbaum, Donald; Turk, Dennis C.. *Facilitating Treatment Adherence: A Practitioner's Guiodebook,* New York:P Plenum Press. (1987).

Mountrose, Phillip & Jane (2000); *Getting Thru to Your Emotions with EFT: Tap into Your Hidden Potential with the EMOTIONAL FREEDOM TECHNIQUE*; Holistic Communications, Sacramento, CA.

Morre, Rudy Rae, *'I Ain't Lyin'! The Unexpurgated Truth about Rudy Ray Moore. Living Blues* # 157, May/June, 2001.

Pert, Candace, PhD. *Molecules of Emotion: The Science Behind Mind/Body Medicine.*

Senge, P. M. *The Fifth Discipline. The art and practice of the learning organization*, London: Random House. (1990).

Schiffer – Author of "Two Minds – The Revolutionary Science of Dual Brain Psychology.

Wilson, Colin; *New Pathways in Psychology: Maslow and the Post-Freudian Revolution* (1972).

Wilson, Larry. *Play to Win: Choosing Growth Over Fear in Work and Life,* Austin, Texas: Bard Press (1998).

Periodicals

Interhemispheric relationships: the neocortical commissures; syndromes of hemisphere disconnection. R.W. Sperry, M.S. Gazzaniga, and J.E. Bogen. In *Handbook Clin. Neurol.* P. J. Vinken and G.W. Bruyn (Eds.), Amsterdam: North-Holland Publishing Co. 4: 273-290 (1969).

Made in the USA
San Bernardino, CA
12 August 2018